S0-AFF-541

IMPROVE YOUR GRADES

HOW TO BECOME AN HONOR STUDENT

Veltisezar Bautista

Bookhaus Publishers

Warren, MI 48092-6113

U.S.A.

Publisher's Cataloging-in-Publication
(Provided by Quality Books, Inc.)

Bautista, Veltisezar B., 1933-
    Improve your grades : how to become an honor
student / Veltisezar Bautista. -- 3rd ed.
    p. cm.
    Includes bibliographical references.
    LCCN: 00-91890
    ISBN: 0-931613-16-7

    1. Study skills. 2. Learning.   I. Title.

LB1049.B34 2000   371.3'028
                             QBI00-500026

Printed in the United States of America on acid-free paper.

Address inquiries regarding rights and permission to:
Bookhaus Publishers
P.O. Box 1758
Warren, MI 48090-1758
U.S.A.

For orders only call Toll-free 1-800-807-6908

This book is dedicated to
Genoveva Abes-Bautista,
the "light of my life," without whom
I would not have had the courage to resign
from my job to devote my full time
to writing and publishing,

and to my children,
Hubert, Lester, Melvin, Ronald,
and *Janet,*
for their use of the study systems
that helped them to excel in class.

Acknowledgment

To my aunt, Paciencia P. Bal, without whom I could not have gone to school and accomplished my dream of becoming a writer.

To all the teachers of the General Tinio Elementary School and the General Tinio High School in General Tinio, Nueva Ecija, Philippines. The publication of several of my articles in the General Tinio High School's publication, *The Hillsiders,* about 50 years ago, launched my dream of becoming a successful writer. It's now a dream come true.

Illustration Credits: All illustrations in this book, except those on pages 9 and 10, were taken from the clip art books, *Woman: A Pictorial Archive from Nineteenth-Century Sources,* by Jim Harter, *Men: A Pictorial Archive from Nineteenth-Century Sources,* also by Jim Harter, *Children: A Pictorial Archive from Nineteenth Century Sources,* by Carol Belanger Crafton, and *Old Engravings and Illustrations (Volume One: People),* by Dick Sutphen. The first three books were published by Dover Publications, Inc. of New York while the fourth book was produced by Dick Sutphen Studio.

Table of Contents

Foreword

You Can Make High Grades and Be a Success in Life

I know the above is a **bold** statement.

But it's 100% true.

You can make those high marks in high school, be admitted to the college of your choice, and pursue the career you want. Or you can graduate from college with high grades and get a good, high-paying job. But first you must acquire the basic skills you need to study effectively and learn easily, to help you earn high marks and accomplish your dreams.

Colleges and universities, especially the established ones with high standards, have high grade-point requirements. If you don't meet these requirements, you're not in, you're *out,* and the only place you can go is to a low-standard college in your area. Who says getting high grades isn't important?

If you're a graduate of Harvard, Stanford, or any other well-known and prestigious university or college, you don't look for a job; the jobs look for you. But if you're a graduate of a community college with low standards, you may not even land a job at Burger King. The reason is simple: the competition is too keen in the dog-eat-dog job market.

To make high grades, you need to know how the brain works, how it processes information, how you can code information for easy storage and retrieval, how you can learn in the shortest time possible and have free time for fun.

My knowledge isn't based on hearsay. It's based on my own practical experience in studying and taking tests. In my high school and college days, I was an average student. But when I went back to college several years later, while I was raising a family and had a full-time job, I became an honor student after I learned basic skills and used study and test-taking techniques. The same techniques were used (and are still used) by my children, one of whom graduated *summa cum laude* from the University of Michigan.

I've put all the tricks of the trade, ins and outs, tips and secrets into this power-packed book *Improve Your Grades: A Practical Guide to Academic Excellence.*

Flip through this compact book and you'll discover how easy it is to read. It's even illustrated with some funny-looking drawings that will make you smile — or frown. And the beauty of it is that it covers every subject you need.

Time and again, surveys have shown that those who made high grades in school, whether in high school or in college, are more successful in life than those who didn't do well in class. In this book you'll learn how to set goals and launch your dreams. You'll find it easy to comprehend what you read, and you'll remember what you learned. You'll also read the case histories of average individuals who made good in school, pursuing and fulfilling their dreams through courage, perseverance, and determination. You can do it, too. You may have all the money in the world, but you won't be admitted by the college or university of your choice and pursue the career you dream of if you don't make high marks on exams. It doesn't matter whether you're a United States citizen or an immigrant, man or woman, black or white, brown or yellow; you name it. It's your grades that count.

I'm thrilled with what this book will do for you. I want to help you make high grades and be admitted by the college of your choice or get the well-paying job you want and be a success in life.

Just think what being a top student in class will mean to you. No more worrying about C's or D's. No more worrying about where and how you can enter the career of your choice. You'll have it made!

But as I've said, making high grades is essential. This book is based on my success, on my children's success, on the systems I've worked out, and on systems used by other people. Here are the sure-fire systems, the very systems I want to share with you now. Use them and you can't fail!

Veltisezar B. Bautista
Author

Part I

Introduction

Intelligence: Inherited or Acquired?
The Brain: The Seat of Intelligence
Prepare to Make High Grades

Intelligence: 1 Inherited or Acquired?

What is intelligence? Is it inborn or can it be acquired? According to Webster's *New Twentieth Century Dictionary*, intelligence is "the ability to learn or understand from experience; the ability to acquire and retain knowledge."

How is knowledge acquired? By reading, by oral instructions, by listening to the radio, and by other means of communication. That's why you were taught the alphabet as soon as you were able to understand and speak your language, so that you could go to school and learn to read and write.

How is intelligence measured? Since the early 1900s, intelligence tests have been developed by psychologists. These tests are for individuals of all ages and for every mental level. In the early years of this century, Alfred Binet, a French psychologist, was commissioned by his country's minister of public education to develop a technique for measuring intelligence so that children who had difficulty in regular classes could be identified and given some form of specific education. A revised version, the Stanford-Binet scale for children, includes 62 items graded in difficulty for different ages. For instance, five-year-olds must identify two easy words from a list of 45 words; 10-year-olds must do the hardest tasks asked of them in accordance with their age.

Tests

The Stanford-Binet does not test knowledge, but it involves problem solving and spatial relationships, using methods that are similar to games. Most children score between 90 and 110 on the Standford-Binet, the equivalent of an "average" IQ. The gifted score over 125; the most gifted score above 130. Those with IQs over 155 are considered to be highly gifted.

The Adult Intelligence Scale is used widely for people over 15 years old. In this test, there are two groups of questions: one for language skills and the other for nonverbal skills such as arithmetic.

In scoring intelligence tests, 100 was designated as the average IQ for the population as a whole. Over two-thirds of the population fall within the 85-115 range; the three percent who score below 70 are considered subnormal. Less than one percent of the population scores above 150, which is considered the potential genius level. The score known as *intelligence quotient (IQ)* is the standard tool for representing intelligence.

Are You a Genius?

In schools, IQ tests are given to children to determine whether they are eligible for educational programs for the so-called gifted students. Here are a few students who are considered gifted by educators:

Ten-year-old Kevin Kaliher had an IQ of 169. He scored almost 700 (out of a possible 800) on the math portion of the Scholastic Aptitude Test (SAT); the national average high school score at that time was 467.

Stephen Baccus, with an IQ of 190, scored 760 on the math SAT and 660 on the verbal SAT at the age of 11. In 1983, at the age of 13, he entered law school at the University of Miami, the youngest person ever to be accepted to a law school. Even at his accelerated rate of study, Stephen was bored and restless. He says that school has never been terribly challenging. (That's terrible.) "Learning faster helps a lot," he adds.

Harold Stevenson, professor of psychology at the University of Michigan, in speaking of IQ scores, says, "Westerners, especially Americans, felt these numbers have the same meaning as other scientific data and that children's intelligence could be characterized by number just like blood pressure."

Critics of intelligence tests, however, contend that proponents of the IQ score equate "speed of response or answering" with intelligence, thus sacrificing creativity. Robert J. Steinberg, psychology professor at Yale University, theorizes that the impulsive problem solving emphasized by intelligence tests is less indicative of intelligence than of a reflexive style of reasoning. He says that this kind of thinking must be restudied.

Intelligence and Environment

As faith in these tests decreases, the use of IQ to measure intelligence is being questioned. Many experts believe that major environmental changes can produce significant increases in test scores; in some instances the scores of people over 40 years old decrease. There are two schools of thought regarding the acquiring of intelligence. Some psychologists believe that intelligence is rooted in the genes or in the brain, while others think that the environment contributes a great deal to everyone's intelligence. Most psychologists, however, agree that intelligence has both environmental and neurobiological origins.

Psychologist Steinberg, among others, has little interest in the role of heredity; he conducts studies on how people learn to be intelligent. In particular he believes that intelligence is shown in the way we adapt to change and interact with the environment.

Whether or not your intelligence originates in your genes, environment plays a major part in giving you knowledge and awareness of many things in life.

I was not born a genius. I don't know if I have intelligence rooted in my genes; I've never taken an IQ test. But I do know that my environment didn't provide my mind with enough stimulation to make me smart in my early life. I was born in a different world in a different time; my world and my children's world are far apart. No one can deny that homes are valued places for learning, where many books should be found and where educational matters should be discussed. Such an atmosphere stimulates a child's mind and curiosity, but I lacked all this when I was a child.

My mother died when I was two; my father remarried about that time and I was left in the care of my grandfather and my two aunts.

At home, when I did my homework, there was nobody whom I could ask any questions; I had no elder brother or sister to help me; I was the only kid in the house.

We didn't want our children to experience the life I had had in my childhood. When they were old enough to go to school we enrolled them in private schools because in the Philippines, particularly in Manila, they provide better teaching than the public schools. In the elementary schools they received a good educational foundation, so they did well in school when they came to America; the new educational programs and the new environment challenged their minds. In fact my eldest son, who graduated from elementary school (up to Grade 6) in my homeland, skipped Grades 7 and 8 in Detroit after taking an entrance exam that qualified him to be placed in Grade 9 in Holy Redeemer High School in Detroit. He finished his high school education in only three years.

If your parents did not provide you with books and other reading materials in your early years of schooling, now is the time to catch up with your reading and studying. If you're in a school with low standards, enroll in a better school where there are good teachers and more facilities for learning.

If you transfer from a poor to a good school, you'll be like a seedling uprooted from poor soil and transferred to rich soil to grow big and tall. Environment is important in becoming intelligent. Studies of identical twins raised separately — one in an unstimulating environment and the other in a rich environment — reveal that the twin who was raised in the rich environment usually outscores the other in intelligence tests. Becoming intelligent is based not only on natural talent but also on using study and test-taking strategies and on the length of time spent in studying.

If you think you are not in the right environment to pursue your education, tell your parents that the family should move to where the good schools are. If they don't want to do that, stay where you are and learn how the brain works, and how you can apply the special systems of studying and test taking. You can outdo your classmates and be accepted by the college of your choice.

The Brain: The Seat of Intelligence

2

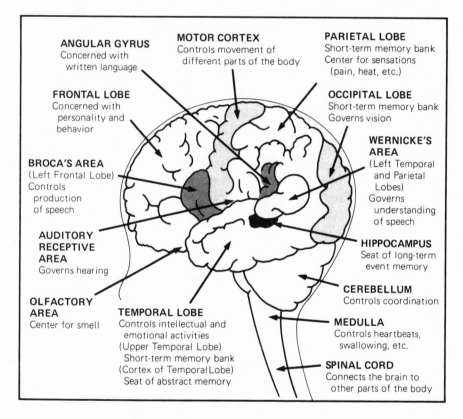

ANGULAR GYRUS
Concerned with
written language

MOTOR CORTEX
Controls movement of
different parts of the body

PARIETAL LOBE
Short-term memory bank
Center for sensations
(pain, heat, etc.)

FRONTAL LOBE
Concerned with
personality and
behavior

OCCIPITAL LOBE
Short-term memory bank
Governs vision

**WERNICKE'S
AREA**
(Left Temporal
and Parietal
Lobes)
Governs
understanding
of speech

BROCA'S AREA
(Left Frontal Lobe)
Controls
production
of speech

**AUDITORY
RECEPTIVE
AREA**
Governs hearing

HIPPOCAMPUS
Seat of long-term
event memory

CEREBELLUM
Controls coordination

**OLFACTORY
AREA**
Center for smell

TEMPORAL LOBE
Controls intellectual and
emotional activities
(Upper Temporal Lobe)
Short-term memory bank
(Cortex of Temporal Lobe)
Seat of abstract memory

MEDULLA
Controls heartbeats,
swallowing, etc.

SPINAL CORD
Connects the brain to
other parts of the body

The Main Divisions of the Brain

The brain, the computer of the human body, consists of about three pints of moist greyish yellow matter and is an amazing, complex mechanism. Though it controls all human activities, it weighs only three pounds, or half as much as a newborn baby. The brain contains 100 billion to one trillion nerve cells; it floats in liquid which acts as its shock absorber. The brain, which serves as the "switchboard" of the whole nervous system, consists of the *gray matter* (the outer cortex of nerve cells) and the *white matter* (the inner mass of nerve cells). It is divided into different compartments where electrical and chemical activities take place, controlled by its self-made codes or by programs like those for a computer.

The Physical Features of the Brain

The brain is divided into three major parts: the *forebrain* or front brain, the *midbrain* or middle brain, and the *hindbrain* or rear brain.

The Forebrain. This section consists mostly of the *cerebrum,* formed by two large hemispheres. In the cerebrum your memory and intelligence thrive; this is where you think, remember, and decide. The *thalamus* is situated in the middle of the brain, above the brainstem; it sends information from ears, nose, eyes, skin, and tongue to the different parts of the body. The *hypothalamus,* located below the thalamus, acts as the relay manager of the nervous system; it is also involved in our emotions.

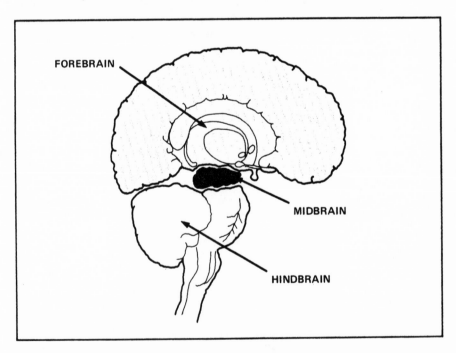

The Three Main Parts of the Brain

The thalamus, covered by four neuron clusters known as *basal ganglia*, helps control the body's movements. The *limbic system*, another part of the cerebrum, is overlapped by the basal ganglia; it largely controls emotions and actions and also takes part in learning and the operation of the short-term memory. The *archicortex (original bark)* and the *paleocortex* (old bark) form the limbic system's outer skin, while the *neocortex* (new bark) covers most of the forebrain.

Each hemisphere in the cerebrum is divided into the *frontal, occipital, temporal, and parietal lobes.* These hemispheres are known as the left brain and the right brain. If you're left-handed, your right brain tends to be dominant; if you're right-handed, your left brain tends to be dominant; some people have mixed dominance.

According to scientists, the left brain governs logical, mathematical, verbal, and written language skills. The right brain controls imagination, spatial and color sensitivity, and emotions. These are generalities, however; many people possess some of these traits on both sides of the brain.

The Midbrain. This portion is situated between the forebrain and the hindbrain on top of a network of nerve threads and nuclei called the *brainstem*, which connects the brain to the spinal cord. The midbrain is the relay station for sensory impulses.

The Hindbrain. This portion forms part of the *pons* and the *medulla*, the brainstem's two lowest communication network stations. These two structures transmit vital messages to and from the spinal cord. Another part, the *cerebellum*, is the largest structure in the hindbrain and the second largest region of the whole brain; it coordinates the body's complex movements.

As you can see, the brain is loaded. It has all the standard equipment, plus all the options. It has power, acceleration, and speed; its capacity is limitless. I've been loading my brain with data since I was born, but I cannot fill it. I can't empty it, either. Amazing!

The Brain-Mind Connection

What is the difference between the brain and the mind? The brain is matter: it can be weighed, dissected, and examined. But how about the mind? Is it spirit? energy? Nobody knows. It's not flesh, it's not bone; it's a mystery!

Scientists can't give the exact location of the mind — I can't, either. They are trying to explain that the brain and the mind operate by separate sets of laws: the former by physical laws, the latter by laws still unknown. They speculate that our thoughts, feelings, and dreams are produced by chemical and electrical impulses in the networks of nerve cells.

The Human Brain and the Computer

Maybe we should compare the human brain with the computer. Both contain wiring: the human brain is wired by intricately laid-out nerve fibers; the computer is wired by metal threads. They are both word processors, and both have two kinds of memory: *short-term* and *long-term*. Your brain's short-term memory keeps track of immediate concerns; for instance, remembering your date at seven that evening or where you put your eyeglasses. Long-term memory stores memories of playing hide-and-seek with the girl or boy who became your playmate in adulthood.

The computer also has *short-term* and *long-term memory*, called *RAM* and *ROM*. RAM stands for *random access memory;* the central processing unit (CPU), the brains of the computer, can add to or take from this memory at any time. When a CPU adds information to memory, the process is called *writing;* when information is taken out, it is called *reading.*

ROM stands for *read only memory.* Although the CPU has access to ROM, ROM cannot be changed: it was "born" with the computer because the manufacturer placed it there. According to an expert on computers, ROM is like a phonograph record because the information is stored permanently, as in long-term memory, while RAM is like a cassette tape on which you can add, delete, or retrieve information, as in short-term memory.

The brain and the computer are alike; it is said that the computer is patterned after the human brain. Now scientists are also studying the computer: they're trying to learn whether there are some principles in the computer's operation that can be applied to the brain.

Input and Output. When you put information into your brain or into your computer, the information is called *input;* when you retrieve information, it is called *output.* It's like depositing and withdrawing money at the bank; without a deposit you can't make a withdrawal. The same is true with the computer. The human brain, however, has feelings. The computer doesn't; it can't fall in and out of love. A human being writes the computer's program, but the brain writes its own. The computer is controlled by "on" and "off" signals, but the brain is always "on" — unless the owner is dead.

In a way, the brain and the mind may be similar to the computer and the software: the brain is the computer and the mind is the software. Without the mind, the brain can't function; without the brain, the mind can't function. They are the two-member team that drives your body.

How Does the Brain Work?

Types of Cells. According to scientists, the brain is governed by two types of cell: *glial* or *neuroglial cells* and nerve cells called *neurons.* The former do much of the basic biochemical work, while the latter perform the brain's main work of processing impulses from sense organs.

Neuroglial Cells. The neuroglial cells help and nourish the neurons. They keep the neurons separated by "gluing" them so that the messages in one neuron do not interfere with those in another. They are the brain's welders.

The Neurons. Each neuron has three main parts: the *cell body,* the *axon,* and the *dendrite.* The cell body is a central nucleus composed of a sticky fluid containing microscopic structures; the axon is a slim "tree trunk" that transmits signals between the cell body and other cells and between other parts of the body and the brain through stations known as *synapses.* The dendrite is a short fiber cable that relays signals to its own cell body. Each neuron receives and transmits information signals through thousands of tiny nerve wires that join it with other neurons in the nervous system. The neurons are divided into different groups, each with its own neurotransmitter.

Neurotransmitters are brain chemicals that control the flow of messages through the synapses over which the messages jump from the axons to waiting dendrites. These are called "handshakes" between neurons. Millions of handshakes make up a single response, thought, or memory. This activity takes place in the cortex, the outer layer of the brain. Here the neurons process the complex stream of information flowing from the sense organs. After being processed, these electrical and chemical messages are relayed by neurons to deeper layers of the cortex, to other brain structures, and to other parts of the body.

Floyd Bloom, a neuroanatomist at the Scripps Clinic in La Jolla, California, believes that perception, memory, and self-awareness become scrambled when brain chemistry goes awry. Once when I was printing out the manuscript of this book, the printer produced strings of letters like *xuelghcwptndkaqklc*. Probably the electrical activity between the computer, the software, and the printer got scrambled. The computer, like the mind, gets crazy too.

How Information Is Processed

According to one theory, input from the senses to the brain first enters the short-term memory, where information is stored as coded sounds of words. New items entering the short-term memory drive out the old ones, as if saying, "Get out of here!" When items are repeated again and again, a process called *rehearsal*, their stay is prolonged and the rehearsed and remembered items move to the long-term memory bank.

Kinds of Long-Term Memory. Scientists divide long term memory into *stimulus-response memory*, *event memory*, and *abstract memory*. Stimulus-response memory makes you salivate when you hear someone say, "Let's eat now!" Event memory may help you remember your childhood, even if you're already in your eighties. Abstract memory has a huge capacity; it stores general knowledge and the meanings of objects and events. It is located in the neocortex, the brain's outer gray layer. Some scientists believe that memory formation involves creating chains of molecules called *peptides* — possibly one for each memory created. These peptides are the brain's microchips.

Data Retrieval System. If you're using a computer and want to store names and addresses, you use codes for input and output. For instance, you may create codes with the first three letters of the last name and the last two numbers of the address, and then save them. To retrieve the same data with another program, you key in the same letters and numbers.

You do the same thing with the brain. You code your ideas by forming codes or key words, and then your brain stores it. I call this process *coding*. You retrieve this information from your long-term memory by using the same codes or key words to help you find and obtain the data. I call this process *decoding. (See* **Coding** and **Decoding,** pages 56 and 60.)

How Data Is Stored

The brain automatically saves information after a number of repetitions. You don't have to save it by hitting the special control keys as you do on the computer. When I want to place data in my brain, I don't say "save"; the information is saved automatically by my biocomputer. The trouble is that I can't delete any information. The more I try to delete, the more I save. In spite of that, I like my brain; it doesn't say, "Disk is full!"

More Facts about the Brain

The brain is immune to pain. When neurosurgeons operate on the brain, it doesn't feel any pain even though it contains a center, (the parietal lobe) for pain, heat, and other sensations. The pain center is the brain's burglar alarm. If somebody tampers with your body or if there's something wrong with the body, it triggers the alarm and you feel pain. But if the the pain center is injured or damaged badly, SOS signals from different parts of the body won't be transmitted to the brain and you won't feel any pain at all. "Good," you may say, but beware! Imagine if your right hand were holding your severed left hand, and you didn't know it!

Size makes no difference. If you have a large brain, you may think you're intelligent, but that isn't necessarily so. In fact, one of the largest brains ever measured belonged to an idiot. An elephant's brain is three and one-half times larger than yours, yet your brain is more powerful; your brain stores more! Intelligence, according to scientists, depends on how nerve cells are laid out and formed; the more complex the twiglike projections from each of the nerve cells, the more intelligent you are.

Brain cells are not replaceable. In other organs of the body, new cells grow to replace those that die. By the time you reach the age of 20, however, thousands of your brain cells die every day. Not only that; the brain shrinks and loses weight, about one gram a year. "I'm already in my sixties!)

Use it or lose it. It is said that the brain uses only 10 percent of its potential. Moreover, if you don't use it, you'll lose it. How do you make it more powerful? By using it through rehearsals (repetitions) and education.

The brain is a drug maker. The brain produces at least 50 psychoactive drugs that affect your brain and your frame of mind. The best known of these drugs are the *endorphins*, which are secreted during strenuous exercise. When you work out as athletes do, you experience the feeling of being up in the clouds, sometimes called a "a runner's high." So don't take drugs to get high. Exercise!

The brain is a clock. Before you sleep, you can concentrate and instruct your brain to wake you up at a certain time. It will do so unless your brain's sleep and arousal systems malfunction. Once I set my bedside alarm clock and my brain's alarm clock for 4 a.m. The alarm clock rang at four; my brain rang at five minutes to four.

You can't do anything about your brain's size, shape, weight, or how it is wired; but you can improve it. Athletes make their bodies healthy and powerful through exercise. You can make your brain powerful by exercising it through thinking, meditating, reasoning, and educating, using the repetitions or rehearsals you need to process information. Code your information and decode it when needed; that is the process of learning.

Prepare to Make High Grades

3

When you enter high school or college, sometimes you have a choice of subjects. If you also have the chance to select a teacher, choose a good one.

Select a teacher or instructor who is a good communicator. What's the use of listening to a teacher if you can't understand what he or she is saying? Choose one who can explain technical terms or meanings in simple language so you can listen better and learn more. If you already have the teacher, you must analyze his or her style of giving lectures and exams.

It's Monday before Tuesday

Select subjects in sequence, particularly in college. Take the lower-level courses before the higher-level courses; if you don't, you'll be in big trouble. If special courses are offered in writing and reading, you can take them to augment your skills. You need good writing skills for essays and reports and you need reading skills to improve your comprehension.

You'll have stiff competition in getting high grades, particularly in college. Many instructors grade on a curve; they find the average of all the grades in the class and distribute their own grades around that average. That means that only a few students receive high grades, the majority get average grades, and a few get failing grades. In other words, you'll be graded in comparison with your classmates, not merely on your score on the test. If there are many smart students in your class, you'll have to double your efforts and your study time to keep up with them. You'll need to beat most of them to make an "A" in the class. If most of your classmates are poor students, however, it will be to your advantage.

Raise Your Hand

Raise your hand if you know the answer to any questions asked by the teacher, instructor, or professor. Show him or her that you know the subject matter and the answer. It's like smiling if you have straight, shiny teeth, or wearing a miniskirt if you are a female with shapely legs. When I was in elementary school, high school, and college, I never raised my hand, even if I knew all the answers. One day during my elementary school years I knew the answer to the teacher's question. Nobody else knew, but I could not raise my hand because I was shy. I whispered the answer to a boy who was seated beside me, and he answered. The boy received a high mark; I didn't.

Because of my attitude and for other reasons, I was considered just an average student. But when I went back to college while holding a full-time job and raising a family, I learned to raise my hand (when I knew the answer) and to speak up. As a result, I made the honor roll for the first time in my life. So raise your hand and be counted!

If you raise your hand and apply the effective study and test-taking techniques contained in this book, you'll make high marks in class and on exams.

Part II

Effective Studying and Test-Taking Techniques

4
Images and Word Codes: The Keys to Memorization

As a student you must have a good memory to retain what you learn at home or in the classroom. There are many dates and formulas, historical events, and other information to remember. If your memory is poor, you may forget even the most significant facts.

How long your stored information stays in short-term or long-term memory depends on how well you memorized it. How effectively you remember or retrieve the information depends on the effectiveness of the memory techniques you use in your input and output operation.

To remember things for a long time, you must be able to use images and word codes that serve as the keys to quick retention and recall. You will store the information in your brain, and later you will recall as needed. This process involves linking of images and word codes or key words to things, events, and people that are already familiar to you.

Centuries ago, when there were no note-taking devices, Greek and Roman orators delivered speeches with the help of memory systems. They associated each idea in a speech with a part of their houses. The opening part of a speech might be linked to the porch, the second idea to the front room, and so on.

The brain can store the information on events easily if the information is transformed into images — pictures that will remain in your imagination for a long time. For instance, in remembering major events in history, you can see the "happenings" as if you were viewing them on a movie screen. You see the characters clothed in the costumes of their time; you see them fighting their opponents with the weapons used in those days.

Concrete Objects

Concrete objects, as in the above examples, can be easily transformed into pictures, but abstract ideas, names of persons or things, and foreign-language vocabulary are hard to picture. In these cases, you also have to use special techniques, which can take the form of rhyme or other devices.

The Letter Code

First provide initials or letters of the alphabet; some form words themselves, others have no meaning in themselves. The letters or initials can stand for organizations or for something else, as in these examples:

IRS: *I*nternal *R*evenue *S*ervice
ASAP: *a*s *s*oon *a*s *p*ossible
PMA: *p*ositive *m*ental *a*ttitude
EENT: *e*ars, *e*yes, *n*ose, *t*hroat
SASE: *s*elf-*a*ddressed, *s*tamped *e*nvelope

Rhyming

You can memorize by putting the information you wish to remember into a rhyme, as in this well-known example:

Thirty days hath September,
April, June, and November,
All the rest have thirty-one...

Sound-Alike Words

To remember new vocabulary or a word in a foreign language, connect it to a word that you already know and which sounds like the new word. Whether you're an American, a Filipino, or a Canadian, you must associate the foreign word with a word in your own language, such as an English word that has a similar sound.

Example:

Spanish Word	Similar English word	Meaning	Word Code Sentence
casa	cash	house	I need cash to buy a house.
mesa	mess	table	This table is a mess.
dinero	dine	money	I'll get money from the bank so we can dine at a restaurant.
ventana	bent	window	I bent one of our windows.

Here are examples of sound-alike words which don't need word code sentences:

Spanish Word	English Meaning
fonografico	phonographic
fosforico	phosphoric
sexo	sex

Remembering Names

To remember names of people or things, you must associate them through comparison or contrast with familiar names and things. If you want to remember a certain person and you can't form an image of him or her, substitute a word or phrase (in your languange, if English is not your first language) to remember the name. You may remember Johnson by thinking of a certain John and his son or by linking the name to a Johnson street in your town or city. You may remember the name Bautista by substituting the name Battista (if you ever heard of him), who was once a dictator of Cuba.

You need to know these techniques in order to remember characters in literature and well-known men and women in history and world affairs.

Remembering Historical Dates and Events

Here are two examples:

Event and Date	Retrieval Word Codes
1864: Abraham Lincoln reelected President of the United States.	I dreamed of Lincoln in 64 (1964) when my oldest son was two years old.
1870: Italians entered Rome and named it their capital city.	It was in 70 (1970) when I visited Rome.

In these examples, I used the so-called link system. In this way I have to remember only the last two digits because it is understood that these events could not have happened in the 1800's. In other words, I coded 1870 as 1970 because I wasn't alive in 1870, so I could not have visited Rome in that year. Memorize only the last two numbers of a particular date (36, instead of 1836 or 1936), unless, of course, you're talking about the Medieval Ages.

I created the codes and linked the dates with actual or imaginary events in my life. I can't forget them because I related them to things involving myself. Of course, your codes or key words will be different from mine.

In remembering events, picture the actual scenes in your mind, together with the characters from that time in history, and let them play their own parts skillfully. Visualize the dramatic actions step by step. Anything visualized is not easily forgotten. If you're learning about Napoleon Bonaparte engaged in a fierce battle with his enemies, you may see the dashing actor who has played the part of the commanding general in the movies. You view the battle scenes, you hear the soldiers' shouts, you see blood oozing from fallen bodies, and you smell the stench of death in the battlefield.

You may do the same when you want to remember the plot of a story in a play or a novel. When you do that, you actually can memorize the events and remember the characters by associating them with persons you know, dressed in the clothing of their time.

The Number Memory Technique

In *The Memory Book,* authors Harry Lorayne and Jerry Lucas used the so-called "number-alphabet system," which involves the conversion of numbers 1, 2, 3, 4, 5, 6, 7, 8, 9, and 0 into a simple phonetic alphabet. The system is described below.

---

1 = *t* or *d*. A typewritten small *t has one* downstroke.

2 = *n*. A typewritten small *n* has *two* downstrokes.

3 = *m*. A typewritten small *m* has *three* downstrokes.

4 = *r*. The word four ends with an *r*.

5 = *l*. The *five* fingers, thumb out, form an *l*.

6 = *j, sh, ch,* soft *g*. A 6 and a capital *j* are almost mirror images.

7 = *k*, hard *c*, hard *g*. You can make a capital *k* with two 7's

8 = *f, v, ph*. An 8 and a handwritten *f* look similar 𝟪𝟪.

9 = *p* or *b*. A 9 and a *p* are mirror images ٩P.

0 = *z, s,* soft *c*. The first sound in the word zero is *z*.

A few rules: The vowels, *a, e, i, o, u,* have no value whatsoever in the phonetic alphabet; they are disregarded. So the letters *w, h,* and *y.* The only time that *h* is important is when it follows certain consonants, changing the sound. Also, although this is rarely used, the *th* sound will for our purposes be the same as the *t* sound: *th* = 1.

Silent letters are disregarded. The word *knee* would transpose to 2 in the phonetic alphabet, not 72. Remember, we are interested in the sound, not the letter. There is a *k* in that word, but it is silent; it makes no sound and therefore has no value. The word *bomb* transposes to 93, not 939; the last *b* is silent. The beauty of this, if you'll forgive our saying so, is that it doesn't even matter whether or not you pronounce (or read) a word correctly. If you happened to speak with an accent, and pronounced that final *b* in *bomb,* you would transpose that word to 939. But since you'd always pronounce it that way, the system would work just as well for you.

How to Remember the Numbers

With these letters you form words that create stories so that you can form images in your mind and remember them. Anything visualized is not forgotten easily. You can do this by combining the consonants with vowels (a, e, i, o, and u), which have no meanings as far as number conversion is concerned. If a word contains a double l, it is equivalent only to one number, namely 5. If the word contains consonants such as *y* or *x,* which are not included in the number-to-letter list, they are not to be changed into letters. You can also create your own number-letter conversion system.

This technique can be used effectively when you memorize long numbers: credit card, telephone, social security, driver's license, and much more. For instance, you may have to memorize the social security number 333717392. First divide the numbers into three or four groups, like this: 333-71-7392. Then turn them into words which may make a sentence and form images.

333 = 3M (Corporation) (m, m, m,)
71 = good (g, d)
7392 = company (c, m, p, n)

Now form the words into a sentence: "The 3M Corporation is a good company." As you can see, the triple 3 is represented by 3M Corporation, the 71 by "good" and 7392 by the word "company."

Vowels and other consonants that do not represent any number have no equivalents in this technique.

My Own System. To memorize two-, three-, or four-digit numbers you can use the above technique or simply associate these numbers with events, persons, numbers, or things.

Some memory experts suggest the use of exaggerated or ridiculous images or pictures.

Here's a   sample of this technique as suggested by a postal book reviewer on techniques for memorizing streets.

"Phillips Ave.
Washington Dr.
Times Square
Salem St.
Pine Needle Ct."

"For instance, picture a mass of Philips screwdrivers churning a washing machine. Fastened to the outside of the washing machine is a large wristwatch. A witch with a wart on her nose (from Salem, of course) checks to see what time it is before flying away on her broomstick, which crashes into a pine tree. Just by originating such a peculiar story, you will not only remember the street names, but the order in which they were placed."

Can you remember the streets through the above description? I tried to remember this information and some street numbers in a short time by forming ridiculous images, but I couldn't. When I do this kind of memorizing, the images blur my thinking. It may work for others; it doesn't for me.

If I were to memorize these street names I would form the following simple sentence:

"My friend, Phillips, went to Washington DC (instead of Dr.) at Times Square to buy a pack of Salems and a pine needle."

I have my own way of memorizing. If I want to memorize names, numbers, or events, I associate them with numbers or names familiar to me so that I can retrieve them instantly from my mind. In order to remember a thing, you need *not* associate it with *ridiculous things* in your mind. You need to associate it with things or images that are already familiar to you and therefore are already in your long-time memory.

To memorize the numbers 12, 14, and 92 according to my own system, I would associate them with numbers, names, and things familiar to me. To memorize 12, I'll remember it as the length of my stay in America; to memorize 14, I'll remember it as the age when I first fell in love; and to memorize 92, I'll remember it as (19)92, the year I'll revisit the Philippines.

My system works. I used it to score 95 to 100% on the U.S. postal exams, which include memory-for-address tests. (This technique is discussed in my best-selling book, *The Book of U.S. Postal Exams.*)

To remember things, you should use codes or key words in storing and retrieving information. You can associate numbers, dates, events, and formulas, with age, weight, height, numbers of floors in buildings, and so on. Associate names with well-known personalities: actors, actresses, politicians, and athletes. Just concentrate when you are putting the data into your head. Don't worry; your head won't explode — it's like a computer. A computer seldom explodes; it just loses its memory.

Other Memory Codes

You can also use the link system to memorize formulas used in math, chemistry, and physics.

All these memory codes involve association — that is, comparing new things, persons, and events with those you know already.

The Link System

When you're memorizing information, take a word or two from each sentence or paragraph and form another sentence or story to link the main and secondary ideas. Here's an example of how to link ideas, culled from a selection titled *Revolution and Independence.* I reduced the selection into four sentences, with key words at the left-hand column. See the original text on pages 57-58. (Reprinted with permission of Glencoe/McGraw-Hill from *Our American Government and Political System,* by Daniel Wit, P. Allan Dionisopoulos, and Con Patsavas, Copyright 1977.)

Causes of the Revolution

Left-Hand Column   *Right-Hand Column*

1. Geographic   1. Separated by 3000 miles of ocean, Great Britain's and the colonies' physical environments differed.

2. Social   2. As a result, two different societies developed, resulting in miscommunications.

3. Economic   3. Britain forced its colonies to supply raw materials and to buy the manufactured goods; colonies also had developed their own economies so they resented trade restrictions, resulting in disputes.

4. Political   4. Britain curtailed political freedom when it imposed taxation, which the colonies resented, claiming "no taxation without representation" (in Parliament).

Now write one sentence to memorize this information, taking a few key words from each sentence. I would create the following sentence:

"GSEP represents different physical environments which produced two societies, two economies, and taxation." (Note: GSEP means geographic, social, economic, political.) The first sentence is represented by "different physical environments," the second by "two societies," the third by "two economies," and the fourth by "taxation." With this single sentence, which I can memorize easily, I can recall the ideas contained in the text.

Enumeration. You can use the link system in memorizing any groups of ideas expressed in sentences and cited chronologically, with numbers (1, 2, 3, 4, 5,), letters (a, b, c, d), or bullets (● ● ● ●).

Some Tips on Memorization

Dr. Sherman P. Kanagy II, who teaches a course on study skills at Purdue University in Westville, Indiana, gives the following memorization tips to readers of *Improve Your Grades.*

- It is always better to understand concepts and formulas as a first step before memorizing them, but memorizing is nonetheless often very helpful in letting your mind make connections between concepts.
- Visualize the words, equations, etc. as you try to memorize them. See diagrams as a whole in your mind and look over different parts of the figure without attempting to describe it in words. For example, instead of trying to memorize the words "When heat is put into a gas, it will expand," visualize heat as red waves entering a gas. Then in your mind, watch the gas expand.
- Before trying to memorize a mass of material, try to identify any relationships that exist between the facts or try to relate the facts to your world view. For example, rather than trying to learn Greek mythology by memorizing the fact that Perseus was the hero, and Andromeda was a virgin chained to the seacoast, reconstruct the Perseus and Andromeda story from the beginning: "In the land of Ethiopia, Andromeda was the beautiful daughter of King Cepheus and Queen Cassiopeia. Andromeda once offended the sea goddesses known as the Nereids by comparing her beauty to theirs. In response ... "
- In biology, it is usually helpful to study systems for classifying organisms (mammals, reptiles, marsupials, etc.) or to learn how organisms are related to each other in evolutionary theory.

5

How to Read Efficiently

If you have to study effectively, you must read efficiently. You must read, comprehend, and digest the information you have gained and store it in your memory bank to retrieve it when you need it. It may be placed either in temporary memory or in the long-term memory bank, depending on what it is about and how you've learned or memorized it. (See **Images and Word Codes,** pages 21-29.)

Six key words or questions are involved in reading or studying: *who? what? where? when? how?* and *why?* They are known in the newspaper world (for short) as the five W's, which in reality, includes an H. Rudyard Kipling, once a journalist, has this to say about them:

> I keep six honest serving men
> (They taught me all I knew);
> Their names are *What* and *Why* and *When*
> and *How* and *Where* and *Who.*

If you intend to be a good reader, you must find answers to these questions because they will apply to every subject you read.

There are four types of reading: *previewing, skimming, scanning,* and *digesting. Who, what, where,* and *when* may tell you to preview and skim; *how* and *why* to scan; *how* and *why* with directive words such as *compare, define, explain,* and *describe* to digest.

■ **Previewing.** Previewing is like overviewing or surveying. If you go to see a movie, *The Brides of Dracula,* for instance, you see a preview of the coming attractions, whether you like it or not, before you see the main feature or attraction. You are given ideas what the coming pictures are all about.

In previewing a book, you read the title, the subtitle, the author's name, the table of contents, **bold**faced headings, subheadings, the introduction, the afterword, the appendix, the index, and some of the maps, graphs, charts, and illustrations.

Previewing is especially useful for getting a general idea of nonfiction books, magazine or newspaper articles, and business reports. For example, you can preview a 250-page nonfiction book in an hour. In doing so, you may skip paragraphs or pages; you may read only the *first two* or *three paragraphs* of a chapter, but at least you must read the *last two* or *three paragraphs* to see what the conclusion is. If the book has a summary or a review, read it, too. For instance, whenever my wife asks me to go to a shopping mall, I usually tell her, "Okay, go shopping now. Meet me at Dalton's or at Walden's." While she goes shopping, I go to the bookstore, do a little browsing, and buy a nonfiction book, usually of the how-to type. While I while away the time, I preview the book, skipping some paragraphs and pages and reading parts or whole paragraphs of sections that interest me. I finish the previewing in an hour.

While previewing doesn't give all the details, it does keep you from spending your time on things that the author wrote but that you don't want to read.

Previewing Is like Overviewing

■ **Skimming.** *Skimming* is reading quickly and lightly, searching for factual information that will lead to answers to the questions *who? what? where?* and *when?* (Who were the people involved? What really happened? Where did it happen? When did it happen?) When you skim, your eyes move quickly down the columns of printed matter, as if they were vacuum cleaners looking for objects to devour. You search for a key word or two in each paragraph that will answer the questions that you want to have answered. Of course, when you skim, you have already a little understanding or comprehension of the subject matter. When you or I skim an article or book, we'll see different key words; while a certain subject may be important to me, it may not be important to you. In other words, we'll see different key words because we think differently.

■ **Scanning.** *Scanning* is a quick, orderly lookout for key words or phrases that will answers the questions *who? what? where? when? how?* and *why?* with emphasis on the last two. When you scan, your eyes act as magnets, sweeping across each paragraph to find the key words and phrases that will give the information you're seeking. Your reading will be slower than in skimming, and you must look for specific facts. In other words, you must find some explanations or give some reasons. Look at subheadings, words and phrases printed in **bold** type and *italics*, and one or two key words in each paragraph. Scanning gives you more information than skimming; but as in skimming, your comprehension or understanding of the subject matter is slight. In scanning, you interpret ideas and thoughts that can create relationships between things, facts, or events. In doing so, you also predict relationships while looking for the answers to your questions.

■ **Digesting.** This is the *slowest* type of reading; you must grasp ideas and thoughts, do analytical thinking, and interpret the *hows* and *whys* in addition to answering the *who, what, where,* and *when* questions. You must read thoroughly enough to be able to *evaluate, describe,* or *interpret* places, facts, or events. (see **Essay Type Tests,** pages 122-124.) In this type of reading, you must gather and sort facts and ideas for importance and relationships, and later evaluate those facts and ideas.

In view of these points, you have to look for the main and secondary ideas in each selection or chapter. (See **Main Idea,** page 54.) Some of the signal words or phrases for these ideas are *The* *most important event is......, The major causes of ....are ...., The five types of ....are........... and In a nutshell ......*Look at the maps, graphs, charts, and illustrations which may give you more ideas or may clarify the things discussed. As the saying goes, "A picture is worth a thousand words." In other words, when you do the digesting, you're already storing the digested information into your memory bank. But in *studying*, you don't only *preview, skim, scan,* and *digest;* other processes are involved. (See **How to Study Effectively,** pages 56-64.)

If you follow the steps mentioned above, you can be an efficient reader.

The Poetry Reader

Let me tell you a story about a man who became an efficient reader:

Many years ago, a postmaster got into the habit of leaving mail sacks in his office while he went to read poetry with friends. An inspector found that he refused to open the window of the post office where he worked until he had read all the magazines addressed to his customers.

In 1921 he was fired as a postmaster, but in August 1987 the U.S. Postal Service issued a 22-cent stamp in his honor. He was William Faulkner, the noted author.

How to Increase Your Reading Speed 6

As a student, you must do a lot of reading of textbooks, research material, newspapers, magazines, journals, and even letters from your friends or from persons or companies that bought your name from mailing lists without your permission. There's so much to be read: mountains of papers that you must sort and digest.

Learn how to read fast in order to absorb a lot of information in a short time. Unfortunately there's a mistaken belief, particularly among students, that in order to comprehend what the author is saying, one must read slowly — word by word, line by line, and paragraph by paragraph. This kind of reading may apply to some type of materials, such as physics and chemistry, but not to general reading.

After studying *previewing, skimming, scanning,* and *digesting,* you must do rapid reading, which is faster than the above, (digesting is the slowest). You must change some habits to attain your goal of reading 600 to 1000 words per minute.

Teachers of rapid reading have learned in their studies that people who comprehend best, in most instances, are the rapid readers. Still the slowness in reading is understandable, because people are trained at an early age to read slowly: when you were small and about to go to school for the first time, you first were taught the alphabet and then were forced to read aloud; then you were taught how to read phrases and sentences, moving your lips and saying the words aloud. Then, in about the third or fourth grade, you were taught to read to yourself; that is, reading just through your mind and not with your mouth. When you read aloud, you're *vocalizing,* but when you're reading with your mind you're *subvocalizing.* To avoid these two kinds of vocalizations, don't move your lips; place the tip of your tongue between your teeth. Don't get excited, and don't get scared. You may forget all about it, and before you know it, a portion of your tongue is already hurt or — cut off!

Slow reading is caused by slow perception of what a sentence conveys. If you read correctly, you start from the left, not from the right; your eyes move as if they were scanners sweeping the words; they see symbols, instead of words, and electrical impulses transmit them to the language laboratory in your brain. Then your brain interprets the meaning of these symbols after comparing them with the information already stored in its filing cabinet. When you read words such as "A pit bull slaughtered a 40-year-old man," you see the event in your imagination. But if you read some writing expressed with symbolism and not with the "exact" words, your mind has to interpret the meaning. If it doesn't know how because it can't associate the symbolism with anything familiar in its stockroom, you're stopped in your reading. In that case you must read between the lines.

When you read, sometimes, you back up because you're trying to interpret what the last sentence meant. That's not a good habit! Once, a new coach was appointed to direct the football team for a well-known college. On his first day of practice he told his players, "As your new coach, I want you to be a winning team! I hope we move the ball forward, not backward!"

Sometimes, Read between the Lines

In improving your reading habits, first you must rate your speed in rapid reading. If your rate is between 300 to 350 words per minute, you must take steps to pursue your goal. With practice, patience, and persistence you can increase your speed as you improve your comprehension. As reading experts have said, an adult can read 500 to 1000 words per minute, with comprehension. Actually, an adult doesn't read such number of words. What he or she does is *idea culling;* he or she gets ideas from what he or she is reading.

You don't have to read word by word but phrase by phrase. For instance, a word-by-word beginning reader may read the following sentence as follows:

1. Iran's Khomeini *declares* **war** with **U.S.**

To avoid the world-by-word method, group the words in pair as follows:

2. Iran's Khomeini *declares war* **with U.S.**

To improve your reading further, divide the sentence into the following larger groups of words:

3. Iran's Khoemeini declares *war with U.S.*

However, we don't use only the two-word or three-word technique. Sometimes we have to make a larger group into a phrase. Double speed, triple speed, and multiple speed, when applied to reading, have nothing to do with bicycle speeds; they mean two-word, three-word, and many-word phrases.

Speed and concentration are essential in reading so you must ignore your surroundings. When you're reading in class, don't listen to what your neighbor is asking you, even if you imagine that he is Don Johnson or she is Victoria Principal. Not this time! You're in the midst of reading, which you find enjoyable and worthwhile.

Kinds of Vision

We have two kinds of vision: *macular* and *peripheral.* In reading a phrase such as this:

We live to ● die someday

the eyes focus on an invisible spot in the middle of the phrase; macular vision enables you to see clearly the word or words in the center of the phrase. Peripheral vision lets you see (though less clearly,) the words at both ends of the sentence.

To help give you an idea of the sharpness of your peripheral vision, a group of words is arranged below in the form of a pyramid. Move your eyes vertically, not horizontally.

A
•
woman
•
believed
•
to be the oldest
•
resident of Pennsyl-
•
vania died at Somerset
•
State Hospital at age 111.
•
Fairy Florence Pile, a native
•
of Jefferson Township, Somerset
•
County, had been a resident of the
•
state mental hospital institution for
•
ninety-nine years before her death.

—Pittsburgh Post Gazette

If you were unable to read more than half of the above sentence without any horizontal eye movements, you should practice by reading newspaper stories, for they have narrower columns. This is a good exercise for your eyes.

Idea Culling

I don't think you have to use speed reading when studying. Although some people say they can read 1,500 words per minute, they are not actually doing speed reading; they are just culling ideas from the text. As far as studying is concerned, speed reading is picking ideas from sentences and paragraphs. Sometimes you don't even read phrase by phrase; you just jump from phrase to phrase. Maybe you read faster, but you must not sacrifice comprehension to gain speed.

My eldest son is a fast reader; he can comprehend what he has read just by selecting key words from paragraphs. He doesn't say he can read 1,500 words per minute or tell how many words he reads a minute; he does it his own way. Once he told his mother, "There are only six keys to knowledge: *who, what, when, where, how,* and *why.* If you know the answers to these questions on any subject, you'll be smart." My son's favorite question, then and now, is *Why?*

(My son knew what he was doing. He had been an honor student since the first grade, skipped Grade 7 and 8, finished high school in three years, and completed his four-year college in two years.)

Below is a report on Charlie Chaplin written by my daughter. See how she picked out the key words to remember the main and secondary ideas in every sentence or paragraph.

A Report on Charlie Chaplin

By Janet Bautista

When Charlie Chaplin was a child, he was shy and frustrated and hungry most of the time. But when he was about five years old, a single incident became the turning point in his life.

One day his mother, Hannah Chaplin, a singer on stage, had an inflammation of the throat. Athough she needed to rest, she had to sing on stage. Hannah's voice cracked during her singing, and she could no longer continue to sing because of the commotion from the crowd. The manager told Hannah that he could not pay her and she got mad. But they made a compromise: they would allow Charlie, whom the manager had heard singing backstage, to replace his mother.

Charlie sang a song titled *Jack Jones* in a cockney English accent. The audience liked his performance and he loved it, and so he sang and danced and clowned some more. At one point, he imitated his mother singing an Irish song. He had heard her voice crack while singing it, so he made his voice crack too, thinking that was how it should be sung. The audience went wild with laughter and applause and threw more coins on the stage. That was Chaplin's first appearance as a performer and his mother's last.

Pantomime became the stepping stone to Charles Chaplin's success. He created a character named *Charlie the Tramp*. Charles and Charlie were the same: they had the same childhood background — shy, lonely, and usually frustrated.

Pantomime is an art that stands somewhere between dancing and acting. As a pantomime performer Charlie told stories silently, with gestures of the hands and movements of the feet and body.

In 1912, after producing some stage shows in England, producer Fred Karno took Chaplin and other members of the cast to the United States. The trip was a success, but Karno lost the members of the troupe to the silent movies. Chaplin became a movie star, darting, ducking, chasing, and being chased, all without talking. Most of his characters depicted despair and loneliness, but sometimes they showed happiness. But when the talking movies came, his acting career ended.

Now, line by line, let's list all the single words and group of words circled above, which serve as the key words to summarize the ideas in the report:

Charlie
frustrated
five years
turning point
Hannah
inflammation
throat
voice cracked
sing
crowd. Hannah
got mad
allow Charlie
replace mother
Jack Jones
cockney English
danced
imitated his mother
voice crack
voice crack too
audience
laughter
coins
first appearance
mother's last
pantomime
success
Charlie the Tramp
same childhood
background
Pantomime
dancing, acting
stories silently
hands
body
In 1912
Chaplin
United
States
silent movies

movie star
without
talking
loneliness
talking movies came
career ended

As you can see, my daughter circled mostly nouns and verbs. She eliminated most modifiers in order to remember key words when she discussed the report in front of the class.

In the second version, my daughter strung together several key words, and eliminated some of the circled words in order to digest easily the "meat" of the story:

Charlie, turning point of life at age five
Hannah, inflamation of the throat
voice cracked, could no longer sing
Charlie replaced mother, singing Jack Jones
danced, imitated mother, voice cracked too
audience, laughter and coins
first appearance, mother's last
pantomime, dancing, acting, telling stories silently
1912, Chaplin to U.S., silent movie star
talking movies came, ending career

In the third version, my daughter condensed her report as follows:

Charlie, five. Hannah voice cracked. Replacing mother, Charlie sang, danced, imitated mother. Audience's laughter, coins. Pantomime led to Chaplin's success as a silent movie star; talking movies came, ending career.

Anybody can memorize the above lines which were reduced from ten lines. By memorizing them you can recall the story about Charlie Chaplin.

To aid you in storing these lines, imagine a young Charlie Chaplin replacing his mother as a performer; he is dancing, as coins are thrown onto the stage. After that, imagine the grown-up Chaplin jumping over the sea and landing in the United States, where he performed as a silent movie star.

Listening and Taking Notes in Class

7

If you have read this far, you're listening to me through the printed words in this book, even though you don't see me. When your teacher talks, you listen. When your teacher talks, his or her speech is slower than your mind. This is why, when you listen, your mind sometimes goes out the window and flies to many places: you daydream and forget all about the lecture. If this happens, you'll miss the ideas presented in the day's lecture.

For this reason, you must slow down your thinking to match the teacher's speaking speed and to digest what he's saying.

Sit in the Front. If other people beat you to the front, try to take a seat in the second, third, fourth or fifth row (if you're not seated in alphabetical order). But chances are you'll get a seat in the front row, because students generally hate to sit there. They're afraid that the teacher may often ask them questions, so most of them sit in the middle or in the back.

When you sit in front, you can make a good first impression on the teacher. First impressions last longer. Prove to the teacher that you are there to listen and learn. If you sit in front, your teacher may get to know you well, because he or she always sees you. Also, since you'll be able to hear the teacher's voice clearly, you'll know that he or she can also hear *you* clearly if you have any questions. Don't ask any nonsense questions and don't ask too many questions, because the teacher may think you're dumb.

Use the Senses. Listen through your eyes, your ears, and your mind; your eyes watch the teacher's body language, your ears serve as your microphones, and your mind absorbs and digests what he's talking about. "I've got it! I've got it!" your ears might be saying; "That's important! That's important!" your mind might say. Your senses do what you tell them to do.

Body language. When you listen, take notes. As you know, you don't have to write down everything the teacher says; sometimes he talks about things not related to the subject matter: how he lost money in the stock market, how he had a wonderful time with his wife on their trip to Africa, or whatever. You need to write down only the main or secondary ideas and associate some key words to connect these ideas. Watch the teacher's body language, and you'll know which points are important and which aren't.

If the teacher looks out of the window while lecturing, that means, "This is not important!" When he writes on the blackboard, that means, "Write this down, I'll ask about it in the test tomorrow." When he raises his voice, when he gesticulates, when he looks straight at the class, that means, "When I talk, you listen...or else you're dead!"

While you're listening, you must ask yourself questions and answer them; if you can't answer, ask the teacher. That means you didn't understand something he said.

Don't miss a class. Don't be absent except when you are sick. Of course you can have someone tape the lecture, or you can copy notes from any of your friends or classmates. But when you hear a tape, you won't see the teacher's body language, you won't hear the tone of voice that indicates the importance of the ideas.

When Your Teacher Talks, You Listen....

Vocabulary. Listen to the teacher's vocabulary, and you'll know what should be and should not be written down. Listen to these phrases: *The main causes of ....., The most important events during the revolution..., Some of the reasons why...., The downfall of Ferdinand Marcos was caused by....* If your teacher says these things, say to yourself: "Hold it! Hold it! I'll write it down!"

When you listen and take notes, your mind grasps the gist of the subject matter. Write down the main points and subpoints, and include the necessary key words, so that you can review them after class, at home or anywhere, anytime at your convenience. You can compare your notes with those in the textbooks if they are included there.

In note taking, it doesn't matter whether you write in scribbles, in shorthand, or in any other style, as long as you can read it.

Typical abbreviations:

w/	with
w/o	without
wh/	which
subj	subject
+	plus
&	and
ff	following
esp	especially
<	less than
>	more than
indl	industrial
int'l	International
misc	miscellaneous

One of the most effective forms of word abbreviation is the elimination of all the vowels (and sometimes, some consonants) from any word. Examples:

prk park
ln lane
zlgy zoology
mngnt management
blvd boulevard

Note-Taking System

It's best to use a three-hole, "8 1/2 x 11" binder, with loose-leaf paper, so that you can add or subtract when you need to. Draw a two-inch margin at the left to leave room for your key words and write your notes in the wide right-hand column, using an outline form that contains major or secondary ideas. After you have taken these notes and memorized them and when you recall the key words from your brain, you'll be reminded of the main ideas or sub-ideas. You can also write on only one side of the ruled paper so that you won't have to flip through the notes. (See **Images and Word Codes,** pages 21-29.)

I have a dream ......
that one day
you will rise up,
top your class
and live out
the true meaning of our creed:
"We hold these truths
to be self-evident,
that all men
are not created equal."

Condensing: Outlining, Summarizing, and Diagramming 8

You do take notes not only in class, but also when you read articles, reports, or books with a view to condensing what you've read. The three types of condensing are: *outlining, summarizing,* and *diagramming.* You take notes in order to get a gist of the subject matter; you write it down for easy learning and fast recall.

When you outline, summarize, or diagram, use your own words in taking down the author's main and secondary ideas. By doing this you can create your own codes or key words in order to retrieve the information easily from your memory bank. (See **Images and Word Codes,** pages 21-29.)

How to Make an Outline

In note taking or writing an essay you need to make an outline so that you can see the breakdown of ideas in sequence. Generally you may use the standard outline form; that is, use numbers and letters, combined with spacing and indentation to show topic headings and subheadings in their proper order and relationship. In this arrangement the major, equal, and subordinate topics are ranked in importance.

The standard outline form uses Roman numerals (I, II, III, etc.), capital letters (A, B, C, D), Arabic numerals (1, 2, 3, 4), and lower-case letters (a, b, c, d).

Make the outline in the following way:

Title

I. First major topic
  A. First subtopic of I
    1. First subtopic of A
      a. First subtopic of 1
      b. Second subtopic of 1
    2. Second subtopic of A
      a. First subtopic of 2
      b. Second subtopic of 2
  B. Second subtopic of I
    (and so on)

II. Second major topic
  A. (and so on)

Below is an example of an outline I made based on a selection titled *Revolution and Independence.* See a part of the selection on pages 57-58. (Reprinted with permission of Glencoe/McGraw-Hill from *Our American Government and Political System,* by Daniel Wit, P. Allan Dionisopoulos, and Con Patsavas. Copyright 1977.)

Revolution and Independence

I. Causes
  A. Geographic
    1. The separation of the colonies and Britain by 3000 miles of ocean
    2. The difference between physical environment in the colonies and that in Britain
  B. Social
    1. The failure of the two colonies to know each other's needs
    2. The failure of the two societies to communicate with each other
  C. Economic
    1. The development of two strong economies
    2. The restrictions on the colonies' trade as a result of Britain's regulation that they supply raw materials and buy back manufactured British goods

D. Political
 1. The denial of political freedom to colonies
 2. The protest of colonies against taxation, making "no taxation without representation" (in Parliament) their slogan

II. Early Revolutionary Government

A. The meeting of delegates from nine colonies to protest against the Stamp Act, a form of taxation, and other laws passed by Parliament
 1. The formation of committees of correspondence in every colony to organize resistance against British policies
 2. The increase in the number of colonies that supported the movement for independence
B. The Parliament's passage of laws penalizing colonies for their resistance
 1. The holding of the First Continental Congress on September 5, 1774 to draft a Declaration of Rights
 2. The breaking out of fighting between the colonies and British troops
 3. The holding of the Second Continental Congress, which became America's first national government

III. State Governments

A. The Aftermath of the Revolution
 1. The Royal officials' flight from colonies
 2. The Second Continental Congress' plea to all colonies to form state governments, which the latter did

You can also use the standard outline form to show the parts of an organization. Here, you show the various divisions of a business or a government organization from top to bottom, from the president to the lowest level. The purpose of this outline is to describe and differentiate the duties or functions.

You can also use this outline form in classifying things and in doing things.

You can also make an outline when you read your assignment, to provide an easier review at examination time. (Also see **Taking Notes,** Pages 42-46, and **Diagramming,** page 53.)

How to Summarize

Summarizing, unlike *outlining*, is the presentation of the details not included during outlining. It's the process of condensing an article, report, or book into a miniature form that contains the answers to the questions *who, when, where, what, how* and *why*. You must prepare it in an organized format with unity and coherence and write it in a brief, concise manner, with emphasis on clarity. In the summary, the topic sentence, and the main points or ideas and subpoints are linked together in an organized format.

Summarizing is not a process of taking a sentence from one place or another or chopping several words from a sentence or a paragraph. Grasp the major ideas and write them in your own words: disregard all general statements and don't add an opinion of your own. It's like squeezing oranges to get the juice, throwing the pulp and skin into the trash can, and drinking the juice.

How to Summarize

Reducing sentences into short phrases and phrases into words requires a lot of practice. But remember that you need to practice, in any endeavor, whether you're an orator, an actor or actress, or an athlete. When a boxer fights an invisible opponent, he isn't crazy. (If he bumps his head intentionally against a cement wall, that's another story.)

In summarizing, you must pay particular attention to the author's pattern of writing. Some common patterns are indicated by the following:

Listing. When you enumerate things, number them (1, 2, 3, 4, 5...), bullet them (●, ●, ●, ●), or mark them with stars (★, ★, ★, ★), or squares (■, ■, ■, ■). Sometimes you may use words such as *also, then,* or *last,* placing them in front of some sentences or inserting them in the appropriate places.

Chronology. When you state things in the order of time or date, that's chronological order. Separate these events with words such as *when, before, until recently, now,* or *after.*

How to Compare

Comparison and contrast. People, things, and events are sometimes compared and contrasted: their similarities or differences are enumerated. It's like comparing Linda Gray of *Dallas* with Linda Evans of *Dynasty:* the form of their bodies, the shape of their legs or noses, and so on. In reading and summarizing, you must be on the lookout for words such as *similarly, either...or, not*

only, but also, at the same time, as compared to, or *in contrast with.*

Cause and effect. For every effect, there's a cause: where there's smoke, there's fire, or where there's fire, there's smoke. Cause and effect may be indicated by words such as *therefore, because, thus, since,* or *as a result.*

You must be on the lookout for these words. When you see them, say, "Aha, there you are!" Then digest the ideas expressed by these words; they are the meat of the paragraphs or chapters.

If you're having trouble with writing summaries, look for models. When applied to summarizing, models have nothing to do with fashion. I mean that you should look for ideas from the summaries that are contained in encyclopedias, particularly the one-volume and the junior encyclopedias. You'll see ideal examples of summaries: history, biography, and much more. For instance, you are to report on the play, *Romeo and Juliet,* you can find the synopsis in a single-volume encyclopedia. See how it is summarized or how an entire work has been condensed into a few paragraphs.

If you must make a report on a book, such as *The Iliad,* buy a small booklet from a series of summaries such as *Monarch Notes* published by *Monarch Press/Simon & Schuster* of New York, New York, or notes published by *Cliffs Notes,* of Lincoln, Nebraska. It will be well organized, simply written, and clearly narrated, and will include the characters and major events in the story. After that, you can read the whole book if you want; at least you already know the synopsis, and you know what you're reading about. You're reading the book only to learn the complete details and to admire the beauty of the language. My teenage daughter likes to make summaries, but sometimes I don't like her intrusion while I'm watching a TV show. When she says, "That man will get killed," I interrupt: "Don't tell the story."

In summarizing, after you've found the summary in an encyclopedia or a booklet, you can skip several paragraphs or pages of the full-length book. You won't miss anything important in the story. Now, you'll have the time to turn on your TV. (Some people say you should limit your TV watching, but at least you can reward yourself with a 30-minute show, after a few hours of studying. Just as your body needs sleep, your mind needs rest.)

How to Make a Diagram

Diagramming is similar to *outlining,* but instead of the indented A, B, C, 1, 2, 3, and a, b, c, it makes use of graphs or sketches or any form that will present the organization of an article. The way you choose is up to you. Sometimes, it's like the organizational chart of a corporation; sometimes it's like a crossword puzzle, but the answers are already there.

You can use diagramming when you're taking notes during a lecture, because you pick out ideas from what your teacher is saying, and you don't have to write down every word. Write the ideas in your own words.

Here's an example of a diagram I made based on a selection titled *Revolution and Independence.* (See a part of the selection on Pages 79-80.)

Revolution and Independence

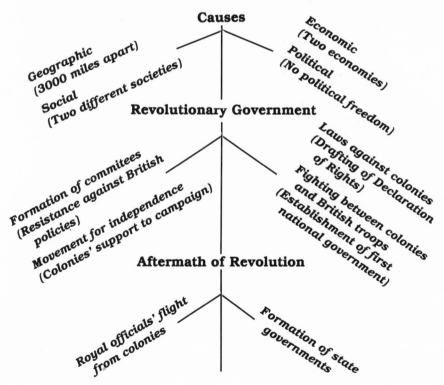

Causes

Geographic (3000 miles apart)

Social (Two different societies)

Economic (Two economies)

Political (No political freedom)

Revolutionary Government

Formation of commitees (Resistance against British policies)

Movement for independence (Colonies' support to campaign)

Laws against colonies (Drafting of Declaration of Rights)

Fighting between colonies and British troops (Establishment of first national government)

Aftermath of Revolution

Royal officials' flight from colonies

Formation of state governments

How to Find the Main Ideas

The main idea is the most important part of a paragraph. Usually you'll recognize it when you ask the questions *who?* and *what?* Such a main point is usually in the beginning of a paragraph. Sometimes facts are presented; sometimes some kind of symbolism is presented, and you must read between the lines.

The author supports the main idea with answers to the questions *how?* and *why?* and sometimes *when?* and *where?* The author will give clues, such as *The major factor......, The main reason......, Most of all......, The central figure......, The most important......,* or *The chief cause ......* When you see any of these words, *remember that they are typical signs of the main idea. In some cases, these words are printed in* **bold**face type, *italics,* or CAPITAL letters; they may be underlined, numbered, or bulleted.

9
How to Study Effectively

When you're given lectures or assignments in the classroom, you're usually advised to study hard, but your teacher never tells you how to do it. You must study in a systematic way: not the hardest way, but the smartest and easiest way. In other words, you must have some kind of study systems so you can learn more in the shortest possible time, storing the information in your memory for a short or a long time or maybe forever, ready to be retrieved as needed.

In 1946 Dr. Francis P. Robinson devised a study system popularly known as the *SQ3R* and discussed it in his book, *Effective Study* (New York: Harper, 1946).The SQ3R method, adopted by many people and even cited in several books on study skills, comprises five steps, namely: *survey, question, read, review,* and *recite.*

Survey. Read the chapter heading and subheads (usually in bold type), introductory and summary paragraphs, and review questions, which usually appear at the end of the chapter.

Question. Ask questions about the chapter heading and subjects, seeking answers to *how* and *why:* ask what the subject matter is all about and look for the important points in the chapters.

Read. Grasp ideas and thoughts from the printed page or your hand-scribbled notes to find answers to your questions, going from one section to another.

Recite. Close your book or notes, close your eyes or look out the window, and recite the items, answering the questions you have asked. You go on to the next section, reading again until you have finished the assignment.

Review. Close your book or notes again, and answer the questions you've asked, giving a general review of the whole assignment. Once in a while open your book or notes to see what you have not learned or memorized.

My Study System

I have a devised an eight-step system of my own, similar to the SQ3R system, but with some additions. I call it *From Here to Classroom Eternity.*

Previewing. Make a general survey of the areas you want to cover. It's like you're seeing a man or a woman for the first time: to know him or her, you consciously or unconsciously take a general look, starting with the head, and looking at the eyes, the nose, and the lips; then your sight moves downward, to the body. Sometimes you may ask: "Can he or she be my friend or not?" "What does he or she think of me?" It's like that in previewing a lesson: you see the chapter and paragraph headings, illustrations, and chapter summaries, which give you an idea of the subject matter.

Speculating. Speculate on the answers to the *who, what, where, when, how,* and *why.* Make it exciting; you'll know the *unknown! (See* **How to Read Efficiently,** pages 30-33.) Now formulate ideas on how you should answer those questions.

Scanning. (Also see **Scanning,** page 32. Scan the assignment in your book, looking for the main ideas in every paragraph and grasping important points that may lead you to answers to your speculation about the subject matter. Let your eyes, (even if they are not the eyes of an E.T.), emit invisible rays that will swoop over the printed words, searching for the answers.

Coding. Now it's time to take textbook notes and combine them with notes taken in class, making a collection of notes. First complete the abbreviated words in your classroom notes. Although this is a laborious task, it is worth the trouble because when you study for exams, you can review your single collection of notes and listen to your taped notes without having to read the textbook.

Also redo any graphs, charts, or equations that you copied in class. These visual aids will help you understand and learn the subject matter more easily. It won't be hard to take textbook notes and combine them with your class notes if you do the job daily, not weekly.

Write key words that will remind you of the main ideas in a paragraph or section. These are key words that link main and secondary ideas. You can use standard spiral notebooks, one for each subject, or you can use a three-hole loose-leaf 8 1/2" by 11" binder so that you can insert loose-leaf paper with new notes, if necessary. Make a two-inch margin on the left with a vertical line; the line divides the margin from the wide space on the right, which should be used for note taking. Write the key words in the left-hand margin and write the notes in the right-hand column, giving the main ideas or points and the secondary ideas or sub-points in chronological order if possible.

In writing notes, look out for phrases such as *The main causes...... The most important events..... The similarities and differences.* These and other phrases will warn you that you are coming to the main and secondary ideas in a paragraph or section.

Be sure that your key words are linked with the ideas presented in the right-hand column so that you can memorize them easily.

Take notes on dates, places, persons, things, and events that will answer the five Ws and the H. Take notes on the **bold** and *italicized* words or phrases in the text.

Below is a selection *Revolution and Independence.* (Reprinted with permission of Glencoe/McGraw-Hill from *Our American Government and Political System* by Daniel Wit, P. Allan Dionisopoulos, and Con Patsavas. Copyright 1977.) Read the selection to code the main and secondary ideas.

Revolution and Independence

Causes of the Revolution. The exact causes of the American Revolution are the subject of debate among historians. It seems apparent today that there was no one specific cause. Instead, it seems that there were a number of causes, of which some varied in importance from region to region, and even from person to person.

Nevertheless, most social scientists agree that the Revolution occurred because the British government failed to meet what most colonists had come to believe were the needs of the colonial society. A variety of circumstances contributed to that failure. Some were political, but others were either geographic, social, or economic.

For example, Great Britain and its American colonies were separated by some 3000 miles of ocean, and the physical environment in the colonies was much different from that in Great Britain. Partly as a result of such geographic circum-

2   stances, two different societies developed which failed to communicate or to understand each other's needs.

3   Moreover, by the last quarter of the eighteenth century, Great Britain was beginning to develop an industrial economy rather rapidly. Britain's need to have its colonies supply raw materials and buy British manufactured goods led to new restrictions on the colonists' trade. But the colonies had become accustomed to freedom from control, and had developed strong economies of their own—largely agricultural and commercial. Their economic needs differed from those of Great Britain, and they resented restrictions on their trade. Thus neither side understood the economic needs of the other, and disputes arose.

4   Finally, the colonists resented, perhaps most of all, British regulations which they believed violated their political rights—their rights as Englishmen. "No taxation without representation" became a slogan of the colonists. They felt that Parliament had no right to tax them as long as they had no representation in Parliament. At stake was the idea of home rule by the colonial governments. Royal governors who tried to enforce new regulations became symbols of British tyranny. Before long many of the colonists became convinced that they could not regain their basic rights unless they were governed by officials that they, themselves, had chosen.

At first most colonists were interested in self-government, not independence from Great Britain. However, events soon changed this attitude.

As you can see, I underlined some of the important key words in the text to bring out the main ideas. If I were to summarize the text, I would make make the following notes, based on the words I underlined. (Your notes may be different from mine, of course.)

Left-hand Column   Right-hand Column
Causes of the Revolution

1. Geographic   1. Separated by 3000 miles of ocean, Great
                       Britain's and the colonies'physical en-
                       vironments differed.
2. Social   2. As a result, two different societies de-
                       veloped, resulting in miscommunications.
3. Economic   3. Britain forced its colonies to supply raw
                       materials and to buy manufactured goods;
                       colonies had also developed their own econ-
                       omies so they resented trade restrictions,
                       resulting in disputes.
4. Political   4. Britain curtailed political freedom when it
                       imposed taxation, which the colonists re-.
                       sented, claiming "no taxation without
                       representation" (in Parliament).

Now write one sentence to memorize this information, taking a few key words from each sentence. I would create the following sentence:

"GSEP represents different physical environments which produced two societies, two economies, and taxation." (Note: GSEP means *geographic, social, economic, political*. The first sentence is represented by *different physical environments,* the second by *two societies,* the third by *two economies,* and the fourth by *taxation.*

With this single sentence, which I can memorize easily, I can recall the ideas contained in the text. As you can see, the long text has been reduced to four sentences and then to one short sentence.

Memorizing. Now it's time to code the key words and phrases in your memory bank, according to how you linked the key words with the main and secondary ideas. This is the process of memorization, and it won't be hard if you use the effective memory techniques discussed in this book. (See **Images and Word Codes** pages 21-29.)

Decoding. After you've done the memorization, close your notes (the combined notes from the textbook and from class) and start recalling what you've read, reciting the main and secondary ideas. You can do this by decoding the key words first from your memory. Remember, you've coded the information in your memory and now it's time to decode it! Once you recall the key words, you'll be reminded of the major ideas that were linked with them. In case you forget a key word or phrase, open your notes and glance at the key words. Then close them again; if your memorization method is correct, you'll be able to retrieve the information from your head. In other words, memorize the key words well, and recall the main points and subpoints using your own words. Do this, until you've successfully recalled the information from your memory, using the key words as *keys* to your brain.

Reviewing. When you're decoding the information from your memory and reciting the assignment to yourself, sometimes you may forget the key words. You may have a hard time recalling the ideas that are linked to them. If this happens, review again; open your notes and see what particular points you forgot or did not memorize. If you did the decoding successfully, it's time to tape the notes.

Taping. Whether or not you've memorized the notes, record them on a cassette tape, first giving the key words and then linking them with the major ideas and secondary ideas, exactly as they were written on your loose-leaf paper. Listen to the tape, wherever and whenever you have the time, and the ideas will be stored forever in your memory.

Where and When to Study

As my only daughter told me once, all authors of books on study skills recommend the usual place for studying: a well-lighted room with no radio or TV but with desk, books, and other materials for studying. In other words, you must have a study room.

Let me add that there must be an alarm clock, a typewriter, and a bulletin board in your study room. You may write on your bulletin board each day: "Things to do today!" Also you may hang a sign on your door saying, "Do not disturb—studying!" or "Do not disturb—sleeping!" (if you're in your bedroom). If you or your family can afford it, have a computer and a printer, (any brand) so that you can computerize your notes and produce your class themes or reports in as many copies as you want.

Study Time

Make a schedule for studying. Set aside a time for studying, just as you set aside your time for seeing TV shows, eating, and sleeping. Make it a habit to study at the same time every day. You may study before sleeping, or you can wake up at 4 a.m. (as my daughter does) and study before going to school. Devote at least three to five hours of your time to studying.

Sleep Before You Study or Study Before You Sleep

It's not only your stomach that needs food. The brain eats, too; its favorite food is *glucose*, a form of sugar derived from what you eat. Every minute about 1 1/2 pints of blood travel to and from the brain; the brain receives one-fifth of the body's supply of oxygen and blood. Because it can't store glucose, it depends on the blood to supply it with this food, which is burned up and digested by oxygen. When the brain doesn't have enough food, it sends SOS signals, such as headaches, sweating, or fainting.

When you're hungry, you can eat peanuts. It is said that two hours' intense mental work requires no more extra glucose than you can get by eating just one peanut. That's why I advise my children to eat peanuts while studying. I still eat peanuts when I do mental work.

It isn't good to miss breakfast or any other meal when you go to school, and it isn't good to study on an empty stomach, but you shouldn't begin studying after a heavy meal, either. At that time the brain won't have a large supply of blood; much of the blood goes to the stomach to aid in digesting food. If you study immediately after such a meal, you'll get a headache, a signal that the brain doesn't have enough blood. So wait at least a while.

Don't Study Immediately after Eating

Alternative Places to Study

You can also study, not only in a study room or a bedroom, (where you may take a nap before or after you study), but in almost any place, anytime: while watching TV, riding in a car, and standing in line at a bank, or sitting in a doctor's or dentist's office.

Can you study while watching a TV show? Why not? Once, when the Super Bowl was coming up, I didn't want to miss the game, but I had to do some memorization for an employment exam. So I taped the information I needed for the exam and inserted the plug of the tape recorder into my right ear, while my left ear listened to the game. (Of course, my eyes were open, too.) With my left ear I heard, "It's a touchdown!" while my right ear was listening to my "assignment." I enjoyed the game, while I memorized the material needed for the exam the next day. Probably, that's why we have two ears.

Driving a Car

Some writers on study skills don't advise listening to a tape while driving a car, but if your school or workplace is far from your home, you can do a lot of "memorization" by listening to a tape of your notes or assignments. If you can listen to music in a car, I don't see any reason why you can't listen to your notes, even if you're driving. Of course, you have to concentrate on your driving while listening to the tape. Your eyes, like mine, are used for seeing and not for hearing. Anything can be memorized if you hear it over and over with your own "receivers," but if you lack concentration in driving, don't do it. You may land in the hospital, not on the honor roll.

Other Places

You waste a lot of time while you're standing in line to get money from the bank, waiting in the clinic to see your doctor, or jogging with a Walkman. Why not listen to your recorded notes or assignments instead of listening to music, looking at people's faces, talking to somebody, or staring blankly at things as if your mind had gone somewhere else?

Your Eyes, like Mine, Are Used for Seeing

At Night

Some nights you can't go to sleep; you don't know why (I don't know either), but you just can't. Why not listen to your tapes instead of counting sheep? You may not know it, but you're still listening to your tape while you're asleep, so there's no reason why you can't memorize the things you put into your brain to be recalled later.

You can study almost anywhere, anytime, perhaps even while you're trapped in an elevator stuck on the fifteenth floor of a building — unless, of course, you're with Madonna.

How to Study Major Subjects   **10**

Whether you are in grade school, high school, or college, you must use different approaches to studying different subjects. In the United States, the five major high school subject areas are English, mathematics, social studies, science, and foreign languages. Of course, the major areas abroad may differ from country to country.

English

In English you'll study grammar, composition, and literature. You'll improve your knowledge of grammar when you write essays or reports in literature or social studies. In doing so you'll have to be familiar with nouns, verbs, adverbs, adjectives, and other parts of speech.

When you study English, you'll be required to study literature, particularly fiction; you'll also read essays, poetry, and drama. In a novel or short story you must know the plot, setting, or theme; in drama you must know the story line as well as similes, metaphors, and other figures of speech. In an essay you must learn the main and secondary ideas. (See **Main Idea,** page 54.)

Novel, Play, or Short Story

In a novel, play, or short story, you must learn the following, among other things:

Theme: The theme is the subject, moral, or central idea of a novel, play, or short story.

Plot: The plot is the main story of a novel, play, or short story; it is the order in which the author reveals events, introduces his or her characters, and presents the "conflict" or "problem." The story moves along as the characters try to resolve the conflict. The point at which the conflict gets under way is called the "initial moment." After the introduction of characters and the conflict or problem, the author creates incidents to show how the characters cope with the problem. Then comes the other incidents which move the story to the climax and the end.

As a reader, you must know how the author rearranges events and how such events enhance the story.

Characterization: Characterization is the creation of fictitious characters, both major and minor. In characterization, you must know the characters, how they compare with each other in actions or in speech, and what motivates them to perform and speak as they do.

Setting: This is the period or locale in which the action takes place. As a reader, you must evaluate how the setting contributes to suspense and mood of the novel, play, or short story.

Point of View: The point of view is the author's "opinion" or "attitude." The author expresses his or her point of view as the narrator of the novel, play, or short story, or may reveal it through a major or minor character. The author tells the story in the third person (he, she, they), while the character (as the narrator) relates the story in the first person (I).

Style and tone: Through style and tone, the author presents his or her choice of words and the arrangement of those words. The author reveals style through the construction of sentences and dialogue and the use of comparison and contrast, such as similes and metaphors. The author expresses the tone of a work through the choice of the appropriate words to express his or her attitude, as in the tone of voice in a speech.

Total effect: How do the above elements contribute to the total effect and meaning of the novel, play, or short story? How do they contribute to the theme?

Poetry

You can evaluate the total meaning of a poem through your intuition, impulses, and imagination. Since different people have different emotions, you may consider your own impressions when reading poetry as valid responses. Each poet, in order to use "music" in his or her work, makes use of "prosody," a combination of stress patterns and tonal patterns. The fixed stress pattern is called *meter*. A poet uses the nonfixed stress pattern in writing *free verse* in poems.

Poetry will be interesting for you if you know how to analyze the effect and meaning that the poet is trying to convey to the audience. You must be fully aware of the following in order to study and appreciate poetry:

1. Elements

a. Who is the poet? The audience?
b. What is the poet's tone of voice? What is the poet's mood? Can you feel the pain or the ecstasy? Can you hear the poet's thoughts?
c. What are the theme and meaning?
d. What is the pattern of rhythm, sound, and meter? How do they contribute to the poem's effect, symbolism, and meaning?

2. Poetic devices

a. **Irony:** Does the poem give an indication of any attitude or intention opposite to that which is actually stated?
b. **Paradox:** Can you see a statement in the poem that seems self-contradictory but in reality may reveal a truth?
c. **Simile:** Are there words or phrases that state a comparison between essentially unlike things? Does the poet use words such as *like,* or *as?* Example: *Her lips are like a red flower blooming in the midst of spring.*
d. **Metaphor:** Are there words or phrases in the poem that are applied to something to which they are not literally suitable in order to suggest a resemblance? Example: *The heart is the engine of the human body.*
e. **Juxtaposition:** Do any terms or phrases express closeness of one thing to another, in order to compare or contrast them?

3. Total Effect

Has the poem stirred your emotions, sharpened your imagination, or awakened your mind? Has it changed your thoughts and feelings towards things?

Mathematics

You must be familiar with formulas, concepts, and processes. Copy down the problems that your teacher writes on the board and learn how they are solved. Also keep all of your past quizzes and tests; probably the same types of problems will appear on future tests, (See **Numbers and Mathematics,** pages 77-96.)

Science

The sciences that you may study in school are *biology, chemistry,* and *physics.*

Biology: You must be familiar with biological terms and must master the classifications of living things. Use visual aids such as charts, graphs, and diagrams. Read an introductory text for the science you're studying and consult other introductory material on the specific area that is the subject of the course.

Chemistry: As in mathematics, you must learn and memorize the procedures. What you learn in algebra may be applicable to problem solving in chemistry. Learn the formulas; it's a step-by-step procedure.

Physics: As in mathematics and chemistry, physics is an A-B-C operation.

History

History may seem to be a dull subject, but it can be interesting and challenging if you know how to study it. Generally historians have two systems in writing history. Some tend to use narrative as the primary tool of writing history and others tend to use analysis. Still others use a combination of both the narrative and the analytical methods.

Narrative: When historians use the narrative style of writing history, they tell about a story or stories. In doing so, they emphasize what actually happened and how it happened; they name the historical places, the important dates, the major characters involved, and other details.

Analysis: Historians gather and present analytical statistics and evidence to help verify events based on existing documents. They seek historical proof for an event.

To study history, look at the title and the table of contents of the book to see where you can find the "thesis," which is the subject of the book. Sometimes the thesis may be found in the first and the last paragraphs of the preface or conclusion.

In studying history, you'll have to deal with names, dates, events, and ideas. You'll also be required to write some research papers. Gathering historical data involves "the five Ws and the H": *who, what, when, where, why,* and *how.* Use visual aids such as maps, charts, graphs, and diagrams to help you remember dates, ideas, events, and people. (See **Images and Word Codes,** *Remembering Dates and Events,* pages 23-24.)

Foreign Languages

Whether you study English, Spanish, French, or German, you'll have to memorize a lot of grammar and vocabulary.

Here are some hints to help you learn any foreign language:

1. Write the foreign words or phrases on index cards, along with the equivalent in your own language. Review them often during the day.

2. Study the simple words at first. Learning them will encourage you to study the more difficult words.

3. Use audiotapes, if available.

4. Try to converse with your classmates or with any native speakers of the language.

(See **Images and Word Codes: The Keys to Memorization,** *Foreign Languages,* pages 22-23.)

Thomas F. Ewald, a former college instructor who majored in mathematics and minored in chemistry at Michigan State University before earning his bachelor of arts and master of arts degrees in linguistics at Oakland University, (MI), has this suggestion for readers of this book:

> Learning math, chemistry, and foreign language can all be aided tremendously by studying *patterns.* In math and chemistry, a pattern is usually represented by a *formula.* Although the student may memorize the formula, this does not guarantee that he or she understands it. That will come with *using* it! Learning the formula for finding the area of a rectangle, for example $A = lw$ (area = length times width), will be helped by "plugging in" variables and following the problem through to completion. "If the rectangle measures three feet by four feet, how much area is represented?" $A = lw$, so $A = 3$

× 4 = 12. This is a very simple example, of course. The idea is to use the formula several times until you feel confident with it.

In foreign language study, a similar situation holds true. In high school, I just memorized the vocabulary, but in college I watched the grammatical patterns. In German, for example, one may learn the pattern:

Geben Sie mir das Buch, bitte. (Give me the book, please.)

You can become more confident with this pattern by substituting other known German nouns for *Buch:* for example, "Geben Sie mir die Zeitung (newspaper), bitte." This advice is useful when studying with a friend, too. He or she mentions a word in English (or points to an object), and you must use the pattern, always in a complete sentence. Use one pattern several times before going on to another one. That way you will really learn it.

Does it work? Well, I earned C's (barely) in high school, but A's and A+'s in much harder college work!

How to Improve Your Vocabulary

11

We use words to communicate with each other; without words everybody would be communicating with growls, murmurs, and hand signs and body actions. The peoples of the world have different languages with which to communicate among themselves, but speakers of English are fortunate, for English has become a universal language. Whether you are a native-born American, an immigrant from the Philippines, an illegal alien who has become legal, or a refugee from Haiti, you must improve your vocabulary to be a success in school, at work, or in your profession. Linguists estimate that the English language contains more than one million words, making it the largest language on earth, but educators calculate that the average American adult knows only 30,000 to 60,000 of these words.

It is obvious that the more you improve your vocabulary, the more words you'll know, and the more you'll be able to read and to understand what you've read in this information age.

Improve Your Vocabulary

Here are some ways to improve your vocabulary:

■ 1. Read, read, read. Be a "wide-reader." Get into the habit of reading books, newspapers, and even junk mail that says, "You've already won a free trip to Beirut!"

■ 2. Let a dictionary and a thesaurus be your best friends. Consult them whenever you encounter any words unknown to you.

■ 3. Make a list of at least ten difficult words a day; learn their meanings and use them in sentences. After you've memorized the words and their meanings, list them on 3 x 5 index cards and file them in a shoe box or in some other way. In a year, 3,650 new words will be stored in your memory bank. In 20 years you will have accumulated 73,000 new words!

■ 4. Be in the habit of doing crossword puzzles. These brain twisters will force you to learn new words.

Read, Read, Read

■ 5. Study prefixes, suffixes, and roots. Most words are made up of small parts, so try to identify an individual part or parts of a word to gain access to its meaning. Many of the prefixes, suffixes, and roots come from Latin and Greek words; they may seem meaningless in themselves, but they express many things when combined with other forms.

Some Common Prefixes

Prefix	Meaning	Example
ab-	away from	absent
ad-	to, forward	advance
de-	away from	depart
dis-	apart, opposite of	disassemble
in-	into	inside
in- or im-	not	incomplete
		improper
pre-	before	precede
re-	again, back	return
sub-	under, below	submarine
un-	not	unable

Some Common Suffixes

Suffix	Meaning	Example	Meaning
-ac	like, pertaining to	maniac	lunatic, madman
-dom	quality of	freedom	the state of being free
-ee	one on whom an action is performed	donee	one who receives gift or donation
-ment	process of	advancement	act of moving forward
-ose	full of	verbose	full of words

Some Common Roots

Roots	Meaning	Example
annu	year	annually
aqua	water	aquatic
bio	life	biography
fact, fect	do, make	manufacture, affect, effect
manu	hand	manual
port	carry	transport
psyche	mind	psychology
vert	turn	convert

These are only a few of the many words borrowed from Greek and Latin. It's natural to incorporate imported words into English; any language is a growing thing. The word *pizza*, for example, is Italian, and *vodka* is of Russian origin. New words are added while others become obsolete and fade away.

We use these foreign stems and other prefixes and suffixes in analyzing words. We can divide words into different parts to learn their meaning. The secret is knowing "word keys." For example, when we analyze the word *anthropology*, if we know that *anthropo-* means man, and *-logy* means study, we can see that *anthropology* means the *the study of man.*

DANIEL WEBSTER.

He Started It All

The best examples of word keys are discussed expertly in *Instant Vocabulary*, written by Ida Ehrlich, and published by Pocket Books. With this book, you can increase your vocabulary without memorizing long lists of words. The author cites over 250 word keys that can be used to recognize the meanings of even the most complicated words. No matter how difficult they are, many words are made up of simple, recognizable units. Although several books on vocabulary are available. I find *Instant Vocabulary* one of the best books.

Let me give you examples of some keys. Any of the suffixes *-ar*, *-er*, or *-r* means *one who* or *that which.*

Examples:

comput*er* — a machine that computes
work*er* — one who works

un- —This prefix means *not.*

Examples:

*un*able — not having the ability
*un*educated — not learned, without education.
*un*folded — not folded

pan- — this root means *all.*

Examples:

Pan-American — pertaining to all the Americas: North, South, and Central
*pan*human — pertaining to all humanity

pict-, picto — This root means *picture.*

Examples:

*pict*ure — a painting, a photograph, a drawing
*picto*rial — pertaining to pictures or illustrations

multi — This prefix comes from the Latin word *multus,* which means *many* or *much.*

Examples:

*multi*lingual — relating to many languages, speaking many languages
*multi*million — relating to many millions
*multi*farious — diversified, many

-an, -ian —These suffixes mean *native of, relating to.*

Examples:

Grenad*ian* — a native of Grenada
Liby*an* — a native of Libya
Somal*ian* — a native of Somalia
Ethiop*ian* — a native of Ethopia

-ment — This suffix means *act of; state of* or *result of* (an action). A suffix makes a noun out of a verb.

Examples:

content*ment* — the state of being satisfied or contented
align*ment* — The state of being aligned

be- — This prefix adds intensity to a word.

    Examples:
    *be*loved — loved with great intensity
    *be*deck — to cover elaborately
    *be*rate — to scold severely or loudly

As I mentioned before, most prefixes, suffixes, and roots come from Latin and Greek, although some come from other sources. The dictionaries contain hundreds of these elements. Memorize them and learn their meanings, and you'll be able to understand thousands of words, even including those that you see for the first time.

12
Numbers and Mathematics

Numbers and mathematics play an important part in our lives. Still, many people are afraid of mathematical subjects, believing that they are difficult and that only the talented can learn and master them. For this reason a lot of students shy away from mathematics, thus depriving themselves of good careers in engineering, computers, chemistry, and allied fields.

As a student you must master the basic rules and principles of arithmetic and algebraic operations so that you'll do well in math. To solve math problems you must work step by step and remember the symbols, equations, and formulas for each branch of mathematics.

Here are some of the symbols used in math.

$+$, $-$, $\times$, and $\div$ refer to addition, subtraction, multiplication, and division, respectively. Parentheses and brackets are also used to indicate multiplication. Example (8) (9) means 8×9. If a multiplication sign is not needed, the product of x and y is written as xy. Division is usually indicated not by a $\div$ but by a bar. Example: x divided by y is written x/y or a/b.

Some of the other math symbols are as follows:

$=$ means equal to

$\equiv$ means identical to

$>$ means greater than

$<$ means less than

$y \sim x$ means approximately equal, or equal in value, but not identical.

$|$ means "when" or "if." Example $a = 10 \mid b$ equals 15 means "a equals 10 when b equals 15."

An exponent is a small figure placed above and to the right of a symbol:

$4^3 = 4 \times 4 \times 4$.

$x^3 y^3 = xxxyyy$.

77

Sometimes small figures or letters are used as subscripts, but they have no value or meaning: The numbers in 1 and 2 in $a_1 + a_2$ *merely differentiate* a_1 from another, a_2.

How to Find Inspiration

How would you inspire yourself or motivate your child to be a good mathematician?

Think of the life of Archimedes, who became great because of his expert knowledge of mathematics; consider how you can think logically because of your love of math; think how easy it is to study math if you memorize and understand the principles or formulas involved in solving mathematical problems.

Improving Mathematical Ability

At least three major factors can improve mathematical ability:

- Memory
- Strategies
- Practice

Memory. Scientists say that the memory has an unlimited capacity. (See the chapter on memory.) We have incredible brains that record, retain, and replay every bit of information on all subjects, including mathematical problems, formulas, and solutions.

Strategies. Mathematicians have developed simple strategies in solving mathematical problems, particularly in addition, subtraction, multiplication, and division. Those who use these techniques are also good at other mathematical subjects such as algebra and calculus, because we also use addition, subtraction, multiplication, and division in those subjects.

Practice. A boxer shadow boxes; a basketball player takes practice shots; a singer (or nonsinger) sings even in the bathroom. Everyone who wants to excel in something does it, for it has been proved that "practice makes perfect." Above and beyond these three factors, one of the best ways to learn math is to have the will and determination to learn the formulas and procedures for solving problems.

Practice Makes Perfect

The Incredible Story of a Math Teacher

When Jaime Escalante, who arrived in the United States from Bolivia in 1964, began to teach mathematics at Garfield High School in Los Angeles, many of his students started to pass the national advanced test in higher mathematics. In 1982, 18 of Escalante's 89 Garfield seniors passed a calculus test which was so difficult that only two percent of the high school students in the country even attempted it. The test examiners became suspicious of this record, so they required 14 of the 18 students to take another exam under strict security conditions. The examiners expected all the students to fail and be embarrassed, but they didn't. All except two passed.

Escalante was not surprised. His secret?

"The real key is *gana*," he says. In Spanish, *gana* means "desire." Escalante states that kids from slum areas (such as those surrounding Garfield High, in the heart of a Hispanic barrio) already think they are failures even before they start school. But he uses old-fashioned methods to teach algebra, geometry, trigonometry, and calculus. (You see, he does it the old-fashioned way.)

The first thing Escalante does is teach about gana. A sign on his classroom wall says, "*Gana*. That is all you need." He says that every child can be educated and that all he or she needs is the desire — the gana — to learn. Escalante seats the slow learners next to his desk and lets them study for extra hours.

Usually, Escalante signs his students to a "contract" which requires that they undergo a rigorous 30 hours of homework every week, attend his class before and after regular school hours, and go to special sessions on weekends.

"Remember, you must combine your charm, your intuition, and your intelligence with a lot of hard work if you wish to be a success," Escalante advises.

Escalante's graduates have entered prestigious universities such as Harvard, Yale, Princeton, and Stanford. Some of them have landed space-age jobs in high-tech companies such as Jet Propulsion Laboratories.

Because of Escalante's unique way of teaching — combining hard work and the implanting of positive attitudes in his students' minds — his classroom story has been transformed into a movie, *Stand and Deliver*. Edward James Olmos, better known as Lt. Martin Castillo of *Miami Vice*, played the part of Jaime Escalante.

Commenting on Escalante's work, Olmos says, "Last year (1987), Escalante was fourth in the nation passing his kids on Advanced Placement calculus tests. The only schools that beat him were the really big-name science high schools. This year, he has 145 kids in the class. Next year, he'll have over 200..."

You too, can put *gana* to work for yourself or for your child!

Simple Techniques You Can Use

Here are some techniques in addition, subtraction, multiplication, and division.

Addition:

Techniques in addition may be divided into the following categories:

1. Simple left-to-right addition
2. 10-packets
3. Multiples
4. Splitting numbers

$$
\begin{array}{r}
23 \\
+34 \\
\hline
57
\end{array}
$$

Simple left-to-right addition. In above problem, two numbers 23, and 34, are to be added together. The solution is called the "sum."

If the problem is as simple as this, and requires no *carrying*, you can simply add the numbers mentally from left to right—not from right to left, as is taught in school. It's much simpler and faster to add from left to right.

An error in "carrying" is the most common mistake in addition. People either forget to carry the number or forget to add the number being carried.

The secret is to avoid carrying; think of another way. Imagine that you're adding 85 and 57. If you follow the usual procedure, you work in the following number:

$$
\begin{array}{r}
85 \\
+67 \\
\hline
152
\end{array}
$$

In other words, 5 + 7 = 12; put down 2 and carry 1; 8 + 6 = 14 + 1 = 15. The answer is 152.

If you eliminate carrying, the procedure is as follows:

$$
\begin{array}{r}
85 \\
+67 \\
\hline
12 \\
14 \\
\hline
152
\end{array}
$$

In this case, write 12, the sum of the digits in the right-hand column, under the numbers being added (5 and 7). Then write 14, the sum of the digits in the left-hand column (8 and 6), one place to the right, and add the two sums for a total of 152.

10-packets. When you add long columns of numbers, you can use the 10-packet system, which is merely the linking of numbers to give you a series of 10-packets.

$$
\begin{array}{r}
58 \\
71 \\
42 \\
95 \\
51 \\
89 \\
22 \\
55
\end{array}
$$

When adding these numbers, do not mumble to yourself, "8 plus 1 = 9, plus 2 = 11, plus 5 = 16, plus 1 = 17," and so on. There is an easier way. Link the numbers that add up to 10, giving you a series of 10-packets. Make a check mark to indicate the 10-packet and write down the "extra" or leftover number, which is added to the next 10-packet.

For instance, in adding the right-hand column of the numbers given above, add $8 + 1 + 2 = 11$, make a check next to 2, and write 1 (the leftover) to the right; $1 + 5 + 1 + 9 = 16$, make a check next to 9 and write 6 (the leftover) on its right; $6 + 2 + 5 = 13$; make a check next to 5 and write 3 (the leftover) to the right. Hence $10 + 10 + 10$ (three 10-packets) $= 30 + 3$ (the leftover) $= 33$. Carry the 3 to the left-hand column; $3 + 5 + 7 = 15$; put a check before 7, write 5 (the leftover) to the left. Continue adding, following the same procedure. This is how it is done:

$$
\begin{array}{r}
\overset{3}{58} \\
{}_5\!\!\sqrt{\ } \ 71 \\
42\sqrt{}_1 \\
{}_8\!\!\sqrt{\ } \ 95 \\
{}_3\!\!\sqrt{\ } \ 51 \\
{}_1\!\!\sqrt{\ } \ 89\sqrt{}_6 \\
22 \\
\underline{55\sqrt{}_3} \\
483
\end{array}
$$

Multiples. If you have a long column to add, count the various numbers in the column and multiply each number by the number of times it is repeated.

$$
\begin{array}{c}
5 \\
8 \\
7 \\
3 \\
3 \\
9 \\
5 \\
6 \\
8 \\
7 \\
3 \\
8
\end{array}
$$

In the example above, there are two 5's, three 8's, two 7's, three 3's, one 9, and one 6.

Thus the solution is as follows.

$$2 \times 5 = 10$$
$$3 \times 8 = 24$$
$$2 \times 7 = 14$$
$$3 \times 3 = 9$$
$$1 \times 9 = 9$$
$$1 \times 6 = 6$$

Now use the 10-packet system to solve the problem more easily. The correct answer is 72.

Splitting Numbers. Splitting numbers is simply dividing a *difficult* addition problem into small units to make it easier to add.

$$498$$
$$362$$
$$381$$

In this case, the splitting should be done in this manner:

```
 49            8
 36            2
 38            1
___           ___
123            11
+11
____
1241
```

Thus the correct answer is 1241.

Subtraction

There are two major techniques for easier and faster subtraction:

1. Adding
2. Splitting the numbers

Simple subtraction:

$$26$$
$$-5$$
$$21$$

If the subtraction is as simple as this, you can subtract from left to right instead of from right to left.

Adding:

$$
\begin{array}{r}
62 \\
-37 \\
\hline
\end{array}
$$

In this example, however, you have a problem; you cannot subtract 7 from 2. In this situation, you usually do what you are taught in school; you *borrow,* as if you were borrowing money from a friend. So instead of subtracting 7 from 2, you add 10 to 2 to make it 12. Now what does the 6 become? The system says it becomes 5. Why? Because you borrowed 10 instead of 1.

Here's the solution. 12 (originally 2) − 7 = 5; 5 (originally 6) − 3 = 2. The answer is 25.

Here's another way to do this. The number 62 is 60 + 2 but you may consider it as 50 + 12; that is, you may consider "sixty-two" as "fifty-twelve."

$$
\begin{array}{rr}
5 & (12) \\
-3 & 7 \\
\hline
2 & 5
\end{array}
$$

Thus the correct answer is 25.

Splitting numbers. You can also divide difficult subtraction into smaller units to make it easier, as you do in addition.

Take this example:

$$\begin{array}{r} 597 \\ -359 \\ \hline \end{array}$$

Split these numbers as follows:

$$\begin{array}{rr} 59 & 17 \\ -36 & -9 \\ \hline 23 & 8 \end{array}$$

When splitting the numbers, you add 10 to 7 (because 7 is smaller than 9) and add 1 to the number in the next column (5). The correct answer is 238.

This may seem harder at first because you're not used to it, but with practice, you'll usually be able to do the subtraction mentally, without the trouble of writing it out.

— **Split the Numbers**

Other Methods. If you're subtracting from 100, 1,000, 10,000, 100,000, or 1,000,000, don't work from right to left. Start subtracting from the left as follows:

$$\begin{array}{r} 100 \\ -51 \\ \hline \end{array}$$

Subtract 5 from 9, which leaves 4; subtract 1 from 10, which leaves 9. The correct answer is 49.

$$10,000$$
$$-532$$

To subtract 532 from 10,000, subtract 0 from 9, which leaves 9; 5 from 9, which leaves 4; 3 from 9, leaving 6, and 2 from 10 (adding 10 to 0), leaving 8. The correct answer is 9468.

As you can see in the above examples, you work from left to right. Always subtract 1 from each digit, working from left to right, but add 10 to the last digit of the number from which you subtract. Notice, too, that you subtract the lower number only from the zeros and not from the 1, which is part of the 10 that you added. Add zeros to the number up to the farthest-left zero of the higher number which is 0532.

Subtracting Large Numbers

We can subtract large numbers by using a so-called double subtraction and addition system. That is, we make two subtractions and add the sums to get the answer. This system avoids "borrowing," the most common source of mistakes in subtraction. It is used most effective when we subtract numbers mentally.

Example 1:

$114 - 86 = ?$

The solution can be found easily by this method:

$114 - 100 = 14$

$100 - 86 = 14$

Now add 14 and 14. The answer is 28.

Example 2:

What is $85 - 47$?

Solution:

$85 - 50 = 35$

$50 - 47 = 3$

35 plus 3 equals 38.

As in the examples above, we think of a round or an even number to be deducted from the first number (Example 2: $85 - 50$

= 35) Then deduct the second number from the same number you used in the first deduction (50 − 47 = 3). Then add the two answers: 35 + 3 = 38.

Multiplication

In multiplication, you can use three techniques to arrive at fast solutions:

1. Multiplying by 5
2. Multiplying by 10
3. Multiplying by 11

Multiplying by 5. To multiply a number by five, simply multiply it by 10 and divide the result by 2. To multiply 45,760 by 5, multiply it by 10 and then divide by 2. That is, 45,760 times 10 equals 457,600, which, when divided by 2, equals 228,800.

Multiplying by 10. To multiply any number by 10, simply add a zero; to multiply any number by 100, add two zeros. Thus 580 times 10 equals 5,800; 857 times 100 equals 85,700.

Multiplying by 11. If you want to multiply a two-digit number by 11, add the two digits together and place the sum of those digits in the middle of the number. To multiply 81 by 11, for example, split 8 and 1 and place 9, the sum of 8 and 1, between them. The correct answer is 891.

If the digits total more than 10, add 1 to the left-hand digit. For example, if you multiply 87 by 11, split 87 into 8 and 7, totaling 15. Then add 1 to the 8 for a total of 9 and insert the 5 between 9 and the 7. The answer is 957.

To multiply any number ending in zero or zeroes by a multiple of 10, simply follow this example:

340 ×	40 =	13,600	(The multiplicant is 340; the multiplier is 40.)
4,400 ×	800 =	3,520,000	
6,000 ×	4,000 =	24,000,000	

In this kind of multiplication, simply forget the zeroes in both the multiplicand and the multiplier. Then multiply the the two non-zero figures. Then add as many zeroes to the product as there are zeroes in both the multiplicand and the multiplier.

Division

There are at least three shortcuts to easier division:

1. Division by 2
2. Division by 5
3. Division by 10

Division by 2. If you want to divide a number by 2, you can use "group vision." Split the group of digits into small groups, as you did in addition and subtraction. To divide 8,306,422 by 2, split the number in the following manner:

$$8 \quad 30 \quad 6 \quad 42 \quad 2$$

As you can see, the numbers can be divided easily by 2. The solution is 4,153,211.

Division by 5. To divide any number by 5, first divide it by 10 and then multiply by 2. For instance, 636 divided by 10 equals 63.6. When 63.6 is multiplied by 2, the answer is 127.2.

Division by 10 or 100. To divide a number by 10, put a decimal point before the last digit. (If the last digit is a zero, then you don't need the decimal point. Simply remove the zero. To divide 4,630 by 10 for example, put a decimal point before the final zero, making it 463.0. To divide 3,731 by 10, put a decimal point before 1, making it 373.1. To divide a number by 100, put a decimal point before the last two digits; 7,356 divided by 100 is 73.56. You must move any commas involved in the process.

Fractions

A fraction is a combination of numbers consisting of a numerator and a denominator (with a slash or a line between them); the numerator is on top and the denominator is on the bottom. The numerator is divided by the denominator.

Example:

$$\frac{1}{2} \quad \blacktriangleleft \text{Numerator}$$
$$\blacktriangleleft \text{Denominator}$$

If the fractions have the same numerators and different denominators, the fraction with the larger denominator is smaller.

Example:

$$\frac{1}{5} \; < \; \frac{1}{3}$$

On the other hand, if the fractions have the same denominators but different numerators, the fraction with the larger numerator is larger.

Example:

$$\frac{3}{4} \; > \; \frac{1}{4}$$

Comparing Fractions

How can you tell which of two fractions is larger if they have different numerators and different denominators?

Multiply the denominator of the second fraction by the numerator of the first; then multiply the denominator of the first fraction by the numerator of the second.

Example:

$$\frac{3}{8} \quad \times \quad \frac{8}{14}$$

$$\frac{3}{8} \quad \times \quad \frac{8}{14}$$

$$14 \times 3 \qquad 8 \times 8$$

$$\Downarrow \qquad \Downarrow$$

$$42 \qquad 64$$

Because 42 is less than 64, 3/8 (42 in this example) is less than 8/14 (64 in this example).

Conversion of Fractions Into Decimals

Use division in converting fractions into decimals.

Example: Convert 1/2 into a decimal.

Solution:

$$\frac{1}{2} = 2 \overline{)\begin{array}{l} .5 \\ 1.0 \\ \underline{1.0} \end{array}}$$

Why did we divide? Because the rule is to divide the top number (numerator) by the bottom number (denominator).

Conversion of Decimals into Fractions

Just as fractions can be converted into decimals, decimals can be converted into fractions. You can do this by moving the decimal point to the right.

In converting a decimal into a fraction, move the decimal point (if the decimal point comes before a one-digit number) one place to the right and place the number over 10. If the decimal point is followed by two digits, move it two places to the right and place the number over 100. If the decimal point is followed by a three-digit number, move it three places to the right and place the number over 1000.

Example 1: Convert .5 into a fraction.

Solution: Move the decimal point one place to the right; .5 becomes 5. Then place 5 over 10, making it 5/10.

Example 2: Convert .07 into a fraction.

Solution: Move the decimal point two places to the right; .07 becomes 7. Then place 7 over 100, making it 7/100.

Example 3: Convert .145 into a fraction.

Solution: Move the decimal point three places to the right; .145 becomes 145. Then place 145 over 1000, making it 145/1000.

Adding Fractions

Add fractions in this way:

Example:
$$\frac{3}{4} \; + \; \frac{7}{8} \; ?$$

Solution:
$$\frac{3}{4} \searrow \times \frac{7}{8}$$

$$3 \times 8 \; + \; 4 \times 7 = \text{Numerator}$$

$$\frac{3}{4} \Rightarrow \times \frac{7}{8}$$

$$4 \times 8 = 32 = \text{Denominator}$$

$$\text{Result} = \frac{\text{Numerator}}{\text{Denominator}} \quad \frac{(3 \times 8) + (4 \times 7)}{32} \quad \frac{52}{32} = 1\frac{20}{32} = 1\frac{5}{8}$$

As you can see, we multiplied numerator 3 by denominator 8, which equal 24. Then we multiplied denominator 4 (first fraction) by numerator 7 (second fraction), which equal 28. Next we added

24 and 28, which equal 52. We found the denominator by multi-plying the denominators of both fractions, (4 and 8), which equal 32. Then we divided 52 by 32 and got 1 $20/32$.

Subtracting Fractions

Example 1:

$$\frac{7}{8} \quad - \quad \frac{3}{4} \quad ?$$

Solution:

$$\frac{7}{8} \quad \times \quad \frac{3}{4}$$

$$28 \quad - \quad 24 \; = \; 4 \; = \; \text{Numerator}$$

$$\frac{7}{8} \quad \times \quad \frac{3}{4}$$

$$32 \; = \; \text{Denominator}$$

$$\text{Result} \; = \; \frac{\text{Numerator}}{\text{Denominator}} \; = \; \frac{4}{32} \; = \; \frac{1}{8}$$

Here we reduced 4/32 into the lowest possible figures (4 divided by 4 = 1 and 32 divided by 4 = 8). Thus, 4/32 became 1/8.

Example 2:

Problem: What is $4 - \frac{1}{6}$?

Solution:

$$\text{Write 4 as } \frac{4}{1}$$

$$\frac{4}{1} \quad - \quad \frac{1}{6} = \frac{4}{1} \quad - \quad \frac{1}{6}$$

$$24 - 1 = 23 = \text{Numerator}$$
$$1 \times 6 = 6 = \text{Denominator}$$

As you can see, we multiplied the numerator of the first fraction by the denominator of the other fraction to get 24; we multiplied 1 by 1, which is 1; thus 24 - 1 equals 23, which became the numerator. Then we multiplied the denominators of the two fractions, (1 × 6 = 6), which became the denominator. Finally, we divided 23 by 6.

The answer is $\dfrac{23}{6}$ or $3\dfrac{5}{6}$

Multiplying Fractions

Reduce the fractions before you multiply them.

Example 1:

$$\dfrac{1}{2} \quad \Leftarrow \quad \times \quad \Rightarrow \quad \dfrac{6}{35}$$

Don't multiply 2 by 35. Reduce the fraction as follows:

$$\underset{1}{\dfrac{1}{2}} \quad \times \quad \dfrac{\overset{3}{6}}{35} \quad = \quad \dfrac{3}{35}$$

Example 2:

$$2\dfrac{1}{3} \quad \times \quad 2\dfrac{3}{4}$$

Write 2 ⅓ as a fraction and write 2 ¾ as another fraction; then do the multiplication. You can convert 2 ⅓ into a fraction by following these steps:

$$\overset{\text{Then add}}{\underset{\text{Multiply}}{2\dfrac{1}{3}}}$$

Multiply 3 by 2 + 1 = Numerator

To find the denominator for 2 ⅓:

$$2\dfrac{1}{3} \quad \Rightarrow \quad 3 = \text{Denominator}$$

$$2\overset{+1}{\underset{\times 3}{\dfrac{1}{3}}} \quad = \quad \dfrac{2 \times 3 + 1}{3} = \dfrac{6 + 1}{3} = \dfrac{7}{3} \quad \begin{matrix} \text{Numerator} \\ \text{Denominator} \end{matrix}$$

Then change 2 ¾ in the same way as we changed 2 ⅓.

$$2 \overset{\text{Then add}}{\underset{\text{Multiply}}{\frac{3}{4}}} \qquad 2 \times 4 + 3 = \text{Numerator}$$

Denominator:

$$2 \; \frac{3}{4} \; \rightsquigarrow \; = 4 = \text{Denominator}$$

$$2 \, \overset{+ \, 3}{\underset{\times \, 4}{\frac{}{}}} = \frac{\text{Numerator}}{\text{Denominator}} = \frac{11}{4}$$

$$2 \times 4 + 3 = 11$$

Then multiply:

$$2 \overset{+1}{\underset{\times 3}{\frac{}{}}} \times \; 2 \, \frac{3}{4} = \frac{7}{3} \times \frac{11}{4} = \frac{77}{12} = 6 \, \frac{5}{12}$$

$$2 \times 3 + 1 = 7 \qquad 2 \times 4 + 3 = 11$$

Dividing Fractions

Example:

Problem:

$$\frac{1}{4} \div \frac{1}{8} = \quad ?$$

Solution:

Turn the second fraction upside down and multiply the two fractions.

$$\frac{1}{4} \times \frac{8}{1} = \frac{8}{4} \quad = 2$$

Calculating Percentages

Problem: Five is what percent of 50?

You must remember that a percentage is a number divided by 100. For instance, 30% or 30 percent is 30/100. In finding the percentage, we usually use *division*, but *multiplication* is easier. In the above example, 5 divided by 50 is .10, or 10 percent. When we use *multiplication*, we find what number divided by 100 will be equal to 5/50.

Solution:

$$\frac{5}{50} \times \frac{2}{2} = \frac{10}{100} = 10\% \text{ or } 10 \text{ percent}$$

As you can see, we used a number which, when multiplied by the denominator 50, would equal 100. That number is 2; thus we also placed 2 above the same number. In the final step, $5 \times 2 = 10$.

Example 2:

Problem: Three is what percent of 4?

$$\frac{3}{4} \overset{\Rightarrow}{\underset{\Rightarrow}{\times}} \frac{25}{25} = \frac{75}{100} = 75\% \text{ or } 75 \text{ percent}$$

13
How to Be a Super Speller

Nobody is born a super reader or speller. Every child is taught first by his or her parents to read and spell at an early age, before going to school. Your spelling ability depends largely on what or how your parents or teachers teach you, but it is *you* who can make yourself a super speller.

When you read a lot you see many words, and when you see them often, you remember how they are spelled. As one of my journalism professors said: "To be a good newspaperman, you must read, read, read, and write, write, write." To be a good speller, the same advice holds true.

One way to be a good speller is to have a good vocabulary; you can do it by studying the prefixes, suffixes, and roots of words. You can also memorize words which are difficult to spell. The best way to be a good speller, however, is to study some rules and the exceptions to these rules.

Refugee Girl Becomes a Spelling Superstar

Linn Yann, a young Cambodian refugee girl, had spent almost her entire childhood as a virtual slave on a chain gang. Fate brought her and her family here from Thailand, where they had fled from their war-ravaged country. When she came to America, she knew nobody and spoke not a single word of English. She came to a strange land, uncertain of her future, but she had her American dream: to be a success in America. She thought that the way to do that was to do well in education — the key to success.

Linn said that everything was new to her when she first arrived in America; she had never seen a TV and had never heard a telephone.

But she persisted. At first she spoke words that she could not pronounce, she wrote words that she could not understand, and she read words that she could not spell. "One of my biggest problems was just pronouncing words," she said. "It took me ages to say 'W' and 'B,' but I found watching television was a great help."

"I worked very hard and spent two to three hours of studying after school every day," Linn said.

Later, Linn's teachers in Chattanooga, Tennessee, were amazed at her progress in her classes; she was soon fluent in English. After two years she had caught up with her classmates; she even overtook some of them. At the age of 12 she reached the semifinals of the National Spelling Bee competition. President Reagan even called to encourage her, ("And there you go again," he seemed to have told her). The nation's eyes were on her; the crowd expected her to win.

Lynn had studied English, but in the semifinals, she was given a Mexican word, *enchilada*, to spell. She had never heard of or seen an *enchilada*, and she misspelled the word. But although she didn't reach the finals, to many people she was the spelling bee champion, who rose not from rags to riches, but from obscurity to fame and glory! This is proof that whether you are a native-born American, a refugee, or an immigrant, you can be a super speller if you have the patience, enthusiasm, and will power to study hard and to learn the techniques for spelling.

Verbs That End in -ize or -ise

Thousands of words end in -ize. They are very common words such as Christianize, antagonize, colonize, mechanize, Americanize, victimize, recognize, utilize and individualize.

As you study verbs that end in -ize or -ise, you can make your own rules. For instance, after the letter m and n, you use only -ize, never -ise. (See above examples.)

Only a few words end in ise, so it's important to spend more time on them. Some of the most simple but most confusing words are advise, supervise, advertise, despise, devise, surprise, chastise, and exercise.

You can make a list of verbs that end either in -ize or -ise. If you're in doubt about the correct spelling, of a word, consult the dictionary. If you have a computer, run the disk containing your letter or report or manuscript with Word Plus or Perfect Speller, the computer's spelling champions.

To Double or Not to Double

Often you may be confused about words that should (or should not) have double s, r, p, l, or n. These words can give you double trouble. Again, here are some rules:

Double s (ss): Examples: misspell, misspend, misstate, dissimilar, dissatisfy.

As you can see, all the examples contain double s, because when you attach mis- to the word "spell" it will contain a double s. Other words that start with mis- however, have no double s because the words to which mis- is attached do not start with an s. Examples include misguide, misjudge, misinterpret, and misinform.

When we connect dis to the beginning of a word that starts with letter s the new word contains a double s (ss). Examples include dissatisfy and dissimilar.

Double n (nn): When you attach the suffix -ness to an adjective that ends with an n, the newly formed noun contains double n. Examples include drunkenness, and thinness.

Double l (ll): When you connect -ly to an adjective that already ends in l, the word has a double l (ll). Examples include beautifully, masterfully, and sexually.

Double p (pp) or **double r (rr):** In the case of words with double p, r, or s, it's best just to memorize. These words include embarrassment, harassment, and Mississippi.

ie **or** *ei:* These pairs of vowels are confusing; you can't always figure out whether the *e* or *i* comes first. Of these two combinations, *ie* is the more common, as in bel*ie*f, and rel*ie*f. Words with *ei* include rec*ei*pt, rec*ei*ve, dec*ei*ve, and perc*ei*ve.

Generally, the letter *c* is followed by *-ei*, rather than *-ie.* Here are some rules:

■ If the letter *c* is pronounced as an *s*, as in rec*ei*ve, it is followed by *ei*, not *ie*.

■ In certain words, *ei* is used for the long *e* sound, even if the preceding letter is not *c.* (Examples: s*ei*ze, l*ei*sure, sh*ei*k, prot*ei*n, caff*ei*ne.)

■ Otherwise, *ie* is often used in syllables with long *e* sounds. (Examples: bel*ie*ve, rel*ie*ve, ach*ie*ve.

Double *r (rr),* *t (tt)* **and other double consonants before** *-ed:* Sometimes it's hard to tell whether or not to double the consonant. (As you probably know, the vowels are the letters *a, e, i, o,* and *u. Y* is also used sometimes as a vowel. All the other letters of the alphabet are consonants.)

Rules to remember in doubling a letter before *ed:*

■ The word must end in a single consonant. Examples refer — refe*rr*ed; compel — compe*ll*ed. In the case of the word desis*t* *t* is not doubled because the word ends in two consonants (st).

■ The word must be accented on the last syllable. Example: commi*t* — commi*tt*ed, commi*tt*ing.

■ Double the consonant when adding a suffix that starts with a vowel, as long as the accent on the last syllable of the original word remains on that syllable. Example: occu*r* — occu*rr*ence. Prefer becomes preference, however, because the accent goes back to the first syllable; thus, the *r* is not doubled.

One-Syllable Words
Ending in One Consonant

What should you do with single-syllable words that end in one consonant? Should you double the consonant at the end of the word when you add a suffix? Certainly, yes. The reason is simple: The rules state that when a word ends in a single consonant preceded by a single vowel (not two or more) and when the accent is on the final syllable, the consonant must be doubled. Thus, the consonant is always doubled in a one-syllable word because there's no choice. The first, last and only syllable receives the accent.

Examples: drag — dragged; drug — drugged; drop — dropped; beg — begged; run — runner.

Addition of Suffixes

Are you sometimes confused when you add suffxes, such as -ly, -ness, and -ment to words that end in e?

When you add these suffixes, retain the e. Examples include sincere — sincerely; severe — severely; immediate — immediately; measure — measurement.

When you add -ment to words that end in -dge, the final e is dropped. Example: judge — judgment.

The Dropping of "e"

What do you do when you add -able to words that end in e? Do you drop the e or not? Here are some rules:

- The final e should be retained when words end in -ice or -ge. The purpose of the e is to keep the c and the g "soft" before the a in -able. Examples include notice — noticeable; manage — manageable.
- The final e should be dropped when words ending in e are preceded by any other consonant. Examples include machine — machinable; like — likable.
- If a word ends in an e preceded by a consonant, the final e is dropped before any suffix that starts with a vowel. Examples include drive — driving; like — liking; arrive — arriving; live — living.
- Y is considered a vowel when it is used as a suffix. Therefore the final e, when preceded by a consonant, is dropped before the suffix -y is added. Examples include stone — stony.

The -Able or -Ible Suffixes

These two suffixes are probably the most confusing in the English language.

Things to remember:
- There are more -able than -ible words, so when in doubt, use -able.

- *-Able* is usually added to a complete word but *-ible* is generally added to a root that is not a complete word. Examples: admit — admit*table; regret — regrettable.*
- Drop the final *e* and add *-ible* if a word ends in *-nce, -rce,* or *-uce.* Examples: convince — convinc*ible;* produce — produc*ible;* force — forc*ible.*
- *-Ible* is used when a root word ends in *-nse.* Examples: sense — sen*ible;* defense — defens*ible.*
- Roots that end in *-miss* always take *-ible.* Example: dis*miss —* dismiss*ible.*

No Rules; Just Memorize

You can't always apply rules in spelling because some words are just hard to spell. The first thing to know about these words is the root and the meaning; then you may be able to figure out the correct spelling. If you can't do this, just remember how it looks, memorize it, and associate it with things you know. It will be easier to store it and retrieve it from your own biocomputer.

Some English experts say that the best spellers are those who "take pictures" of words. A good speller, they say, has seen a word correctly and remembers how it's supposed to look.

If They Can, So Can You

Many people have become super spellers. Linn Yann, mentioned in the beginning of this chapter, became a spelling whiz kid. Two of my children won first and third place in a school spelling contest for pupils from fifth to seventh grades.

There was also the case, years ago, of a clerk-typist in a city in California, who became the "walking dictionary" for his office-mates.

I knew this clerk-typist well; it was me. The only thing these spellers did was study spelling. If they can do it, so can you.

Study Prefixes, Suffixes, and Roots of Words

14
Essays: What Are They?

You can enhance your writing skills if you define clearly what an essay is and how to distinguish the different types of essays.

The dictionary defines an essay as a composition on a particular theme or subject, so whatever you write — a theme, a research report, or a story — you're writing an essay. Basically, there are four kinds of essays: *narrative, descriptive, expository,* and *persuasive* or *argumentative.* ·

The Narrative Essay

In a *narrative essay,* narrative writing predominates, though description and exposition also may be used. Narrative writing is used in diaries, feature stories, short stories, and other literary forms.

A narrative essay makes a point or presents a main idea. The subject of the narrative essay is the main point that the writer shares with the readers. For example, a novel may be considered as a series of narrative essays.

Four major factors contribute to a good narrative essay (in a short story for instance): *point of view, pacing, chronology,* and *transitions.*

Point of view: Point of view is the writer's opinion or attitude, as in the question, "What is your point of view on abortion?" In narration the point of view is expressed by whoever is telling the story; this may be any one of the characters.

In a narration, for instance, the following viewpoints may express the writer's thoughts and feelings:

a. *First person:* The story teller expresses only his or her own thoughts and feelings.

b. *Third person omniscient:* The author expresses the thoughts and feelings of any number of characters.

c. *Third person limited omniscient:* The author expresses the thoughts and feelings of only one character.

d. *Third person objective:* The author does not reveal the thoughts and feelings of any of the characters.

Pacing: Pacing pertains to the amount of detail used in the story's parts or scenes. In some cases, every action is told; in others, only the major scenes or actions are emphasized.

Chronology: Chronology is the story's time sequence. Some writers tell the story in chronological sequence — that is, as the story occurs, from beginning to end. Other writers, however, tell the story or novel with flashbacks; they go back to previous events, then return to the present.

Transition: Transition pertains to the types of words, phrases, or sentences used to move from one scene to another, such as *before, earlier, finally, later, next,* and *then.*

The Descriptive Essay

A *descriptive essay* tells about a place, an object, or a person. To give a good description, you have to use all your senses: sight, hearing, taste, smell, and touch. If you're in a city, for instance, what do you see, hear, or smell? What do you feel when you touch the edge of a broken glass with your hands?

In this kind of writing, you have to use figures of speech such as similes and metaphors, to give visual images of what you're describing. In describing a place, for instance, make an outline or a sketch so you can describe the scenery easily. In writing a subjective description, you must choose the proper words and phrases to give the connotations you want to express.

In describing an object, apply some human element to your subject. For instance, a wooden chair may have intricate carvings.

In describing a person, you may do a characterization or a profile. Characterization pertains to the personal qualities of an individual, describing what he or she does and what his character traits are. A profile is a short, interesting biographical sketch in which the writer cites facts and statistics. Usually it includes habits, physical descriptions, personality traits, and anecdotes.

Narration and description complement each other.

The Expository Essay

An *expository essay* exposes or explains the meanings or workings of things. The four major parts or subtypes of exposition are *comparison and contrast, definition, division or classification,* and *cause and effect*; the last type predominates in persuasive essays.

In an expository essay you may also use narration and description to explain fully what you're discussing.

Writers use comparison and contrast to discuss the similarities and differences in two or more things. Definition is used to explain things; division and classification are applied to an object or a set of objects. To prove your point a writer reveals cause and effect.

An expository or explanatory essay may also include simple, step-by-step instructions. How-to books, such as cookbooks and exercise books, are composed of a series of expository essays. They are written in short, simple sentences and paragraphs.

The Persuasive or Argumentative Essay

A *persuasive essay* convinces the reader to do something or believe in something. It also uses all the techniques of narration, description, and exposition.

In a persuasive essay, the writer can achieve his or her goal by appealing to the reader's emotions, by establishing credibility, and by presenting statistical proof and sound judgment to support the argument. The writer also acknowledges and refutes the opposition's arguments or point of view.

When you write a persuasive essay, use different appeals: *emotional, ethical, logical or argumentative,* and *cause and effect.*

In *emotional appeal,* the writer attempts to convince the readers by playing on their emotions.

Ethical appeal involves the presentation of both sides or pros and cons of an issue or argument. After stating both sides you'll still say in the end that you're right and you will have presented valid conclusions to support your appeal.

Logical appeal involves the reader's sense of logic — that is, allowing him or her to draw logical conclusions from logical premises.

Cause and effect involves a series of events or conditions, the last of which could not have happened without the previous ones. In using cause and effect appeal, support your conclusion with evidence such as statistics, surveys, or happenings based on your own and other people's experiences.

How to Write a Theme
or a Research Paper 15

You can write a good *theme* or a *research paper* (which may be a *term paper*) if you organize it properly and write it clearly in an interesting style.

A *theme* is a short, informal essay. Whether it is written in class or at home, the length of the composition depends on your teacher's requirements.

A *research paper* is a study of a subject. It is more complex than a theme in the sense that it requires thorough, accurate research and study of the assigned subject matter. It may be 15 pages long or more, depending upon the complexity of the subject. The theme and the research paper are based on the same format and organization.

The Theme

The three traditional forms of themes are *descriptive, expository* or *explanatory,* and *persuasive* or *argumentative.* The *narrative* style is not usually used in the theme, although narrative paragraphs may be used.

When you compose a theme, you're writing an essay, so when you develop a descriptive theme, for example, you're writing a descriptive essay. (See **Essays: What Are They?** pages 104-107.)

The Introduction

Whatever you're writing about, your theme must contain *three major parts:* the *introduction,* the *body,* and the *conclusion.* In the introduction, you must reveal the subject or meaning of the essay and state your position or point of view.

The beginning paragraphs should be atttention-getting, and should let the reader know where you're leading him or her.

If you're writing a *descriptive theme*, tell the reader what you're going to describe; if you're writing an *expository theme*, reveal what you're going to explain. If you're writing a *persuasive theme*, tell the reader what subject will be debated and what your position will be.

The Body

After writing the opening paragraph or paragraphs, make   a formal or informal outline to develop your ideas for the main body of the theme. List the main points and subpoints, with the use of Arabic numerals and small letters. In an informal outline, you only have to make a "jot outline" similar to the one on page 40.

The body of the theme must contain the specific steps or reasons you're giving to explain things or support your arguments or point of view, particularly in a persuasive theme. You must present your arguments point by point: point 1, point 2, and so on.

The Conclusion

In the conclusion, you restate the thesis or subject matter of the theme and wrapup your point of view on the basis of what you've presented.

The Research Paper

In writing a *research paper*, (which may be a *term paper*) you're writing an expository or a persuasive essay. Hence, it may include narrative, descriptive, expository, or persuasive elements. (See **Essays: What Are They?** pages 104-107.)

You must document all the sources you used to develop your research paper. Like a theme, the research paper must have three major parts: the *introduction*, the *body*, and the *conclusion*.

The topic may be assigned by your teacher, or you may select your own topic, subject to the teacher's approval. If you select your own topic, pick one which is related to your course. Choose a subject which is not too general but not too limited in scope. You should be able to develop this subject into a good research paper, in which you can include plenty of statistics, historical proofs, and strong arguments (particularly if it's a persuasive or an argumentative research report).

Research

The first place to go to in researching a subject is the library. Consult the card catalog for facts about your subject matter. The card catalog is an alphabetical listing of all books and periodicals in the library, kept on 3" x 5" cards. The cards are arranged by authors, by titles, and by subjects. Most of the time, you won't know the authors and titles of books on particular subjects, so you'll rely mostly on cards arranged by subject. Some library catalogs are computerized.

Taking Notes

You may make notes on 3" x 5" index cards or in a spiral-bound notebook. The cards will give you more flexibility because you can always add or rearrange material.

As always, citing facts and figures in outline form, particularly for the body of the research paper, is very important. (See **Condensing: Outlining, Summarizing, and Diagramming,** pages 47-54.) If your paper includes important dates, you may list events in chronological order on index cards. You can also use index cards in preparing the bibliography. The bibliography is written on a page or on separate pages at the end of the work. Examples of bibliography items are as follows:

Bliss, Edwin C. *Doing It Now.*Charles Scribner's Sons, New York.

Book with two authors:

Armstrong, William H. and Willard Lampee II. *Study Tips: How to Study Effectively and Get Better Grades.* Barron's Educational Series, Woodbury, NY.

Magazine:

Reagan, Ron. "To Know a Genius." *Parade Magazine,* October 2, 1983, pp. 23-21.

Newspaper:

Trimer, Margaret. "Moua Yang." *Detroit Free Press,* July 7, 1987. pp. 23-24.

Telephone Interview:

Rodriguez, Ferdinand. Telephone interview, March 10, 1985.

The Outline

You must organize your facts and figures into an outline. (See **Condensing: Outlining, Summarizing, and Diagramming,** pages 47-54.) In that way you'll find it easier to write the introduction, body, and conclusion.

As mentioned earlier in this chapter, you must grab the reader's attention with a catchy paragraph, giving the central theme of the research report and your point of view.

It would be better to cite the above points in the first paragraph, so that you will know how to discuss the subject and end the report.

Then make an outline of the main body of the paper. In this section enumerate the point-by-point arguments or the facts and figures to prove the central theme you stated in the introduction.

After writing the outline, write the conclusion, restating your central theme and wrapping up your point of view on the basis of your research and your personal knowledge and experience.

The Writing Process

After you've written the first paragraph or two, the outline, and the conclusion, it is time to write the report.

Rewrite the introduction, if necessary. Then develop the ideas you listed in the outline, into phrases, sentences, and paragraphs. Your sentences may vary in length, but the important point is to write in a clear, concise, easy-to-understand style.

After writing the body of the paper, rewrite the conclusion, if needed; make sure you have reestablished your thesis and your point of view.

Footnotes

Footnotes are used when you quote an author or when you refer to another author's facts or ideas. You also use footnotes when you use specific figures, charts, graphs, drawings, or pictures from other sources.

Footnotes are placed at the bottom of the page in the body of the paper, as in [1]Mandino, Og. *The Greatest Salesman in the World.* Bantam Books, New York. p. 90.

Remember to number the footnotes consecutively. Place the number of the footnote at the end of the quote or citation. Example: "They felt that Parliament had no right to tax them as long as they had no representation in Parliamant."[1]

Revision

After you have written the first draft of your research paper, you can begin the revision. Here are some guidelines for revising:

1. Use a dictionary and a thesaurus to help you find the exact word you want to use.

2. Delete and substitute words as needed as you select the proper phrases and sentences.

3. Take note of your grammar, spelling, and punctuation.

4. Read the report aloud to hear how your writing sounds.

The Final Draft

If you use a word processor and a printer in writing your report, it will be easy for you to make the final adjustments in your work. If possible, use a letter-quality printer instead of dot matrix.

The title page should include the title of your report, your name, the name of the course, and the date. You should not number the title page.

The first page of the report, with the title in capital letters at the top of the page, should be numbered at the bottom. All succeeding pages, however, should be numbered at the top, in the center or in the upper right-hand corner.

The report should be double spaced, except for the footnotes, the bibliography, and any quotations; these should be single spaced. Proofread your report for typographical and other errors before submitting it to your teacher or professor.

16
How to Make a Speech

When you give a verbal report in front of your class, you're making a speech. If you know the components of a speech, you'll know how to think about it, how to write it, and how to deliver it in the most effective way.

You make a speech in order to inform or teach, to persuade, to command, or to amuse. Your speech may be read, memorized, or delivered extemporaneously.

Parts of a Speech

The parts of a speech are the *opener,* the *content,* and the *closer.* A speech may last three to five minutes, 30 minutes, or as long as one hour, depending on the audience and the occasion. A speech in class, for example, such as a report on the rise and fall of Julius Caesar, may take five to 10 minutes.

Opener: As in writing an essay, you must grab your listeners' attention in the opening or introduction. State the main theme of your talk and express your point of view.

Content: In this portion of the speech, you enumerate the details or the arguments of your report. Cite them point by point in order to persuade or to command. If you wish to inform, cite facts and figures or present step-by-step instructions to your listeners.

Closer: Also see *Conclusion,* **Essays: What Are They?** pages 104-107.) In the closing, you restate your thesis or the point of the speech, and then summarize your point of view with regard to your subject matter.

In speaking, you must combine soft and loud delivery so that your speech will be interesting. Make the necessary pauses in every phrase or sentence, stressing certain words or phrases that you want to emphasize.

Raise your voice, too. Don't make your classmates shout "Louder! Louder!" Don't use your throat to make your voice louder; to produce a stronger voice, push with your abdominal muscles as if you're exhaling.

As you speak, look at your classmates as if you were not seeing them; ignore the surroundings as if you were alone on the beach. Or look at a particular person as if you were talking to him or her. When you do this, you'll forget stage fright and you'll do well in recitation or speaking in front of the class. If you need to practice, why not speak before a video camera and see and hear yourself speaking?

In that way you can improve on the way you speak. After you polish your act before the camera, you can perform the same "act" in front of your classmates. You can also use a tape recorder to record and play your speech.

When you want to make a report you don't read. The best thing to do when you're speaking in front of an audience, is to write the opener and closer and memorize them. You don't need, however, to memorize the body or the content; have that in outline form.

Here's a three-to-five-minute speech that I delivered before a small group of writers and would-be writers. (Please note that the opener and the closer were written to be memorized, while the content is in outline form.)

How to Be Your Own Publisher

Whatever you are, a doctor, an engineer, or a speech pathologist, you can make money selling information through so-called "how-to" books, cassette tapes, or videotapes. All you have to do is solve people's problems by showing them step by step how to improve themselves or to do or make things. You can be a good teacher and you can launch your "how-to" information business by publishing your own books or cassette tapes.

(Outline of Content)

I Been writing and publishing since 1985. Part time first, later quit job. Work two-four hours a day. Books marketed by other companies.

II. You can be a book writer.
   1. Doctor - "How to Be Your Own Doctor"
   2. Auto company employee - "How to Get a Job in an Auto Company"
   3. Speech pathologist - "How to Reduce Your Foreign Accent"
   4. I used my own system. You use your own systems.
       a. "How to Buy a Used Car"
       b. "How to Travel Around the U.S. in 80 Days"

III. Things to do.

   Pinpoint the market. Who is going to buy your books or tapes? To be successful, present your own systems of doing things. Should be different from other books and tapes in the market.

IV. Books, cassettes and videotapes can be produced and reproduced in thousands or even millions of copies.
   1. At $10.00, 50,000 copies = $500,000
   2. At $10.00, 100,000 copies = $1,000,000

In conclusion, I think that anyone of you, if you enjoy writing and teaching people, can be a book, cassette, or videotape publisher. I challenge you to be a writer and/or publisher. In that way you'll help people improve their lives and you'll make money, too. The market is waiting for you!

As you can see, the opener and the closer were written to be memorized, and the content or body is in outline form.

Memorize the opener. To aid you in memorizing, use as keys two or three words of each sentence in the paragraph. For instance, the key words in the introduction to the above speech are: "Whatever you are," "All you have," and "You can be."

In the content or body, the key words to be memorized are (I) "Been writing," (II) "You can be," (III) "Things to do," and (IV) "Books, cassettes, and videotapes."

By memorizing the key words, you'll recall the outline easily.

In the closer of the speech, the key words should be "In conclusion," "I challenge you," "In that way," and "The market is…"

The Link System

To remember the ideas or key words in sequence, you can use the "link system." Take the three or four key words from a sentence or paragraph and link them together and then memorize them. These key words will remind you of every idea in a paragraph or paragraphs. All you have to do is memorize these key words to memorize the report or speech, idea for idea. If you do this, you'll make a good presentation and earn high marks on recitations or reports.

Another Type of Link System

Strategies for Various Types of Examinations 17

All About Tests

As a student, you have to undergo different types of tests to determine what you know or you don't know about a subject, whether it is *biology, physics,* or *history.* Some types of tests are classroom tests, standardized tests, achievement tests, norm-referenced tests, criterion-referenced tests, and aptitude tests.

■ **Classroom tests.** Your teachers give you the classroom tests to find out how much you've learned or unlearned in a day, a week, a month, or a year.

■ **Standardized tests.** Educators give these tests to students in thousands of classrooms at different times under standard conditions; for instance, a certain test must be finished in the same length of time by everyone who takes it. Standardized tests allow the comparison of students in different schools throughout the country; they are also given as entrance examinations.

■ **Achievement tests.** Your teachers use these tests to evaluate what you've learned in a particular subject. In most cases, they consider the final examinations as achievement tests.

■ **Norm-referenced tests.** With these tests you'll know how well you're doing in math or science or reading compared with other students in a norm group, which is a representative sample from a school district, a state, or the nation.

■ **Criterion-referenced tests.** These tests measure what you know rather than how you compare with other students in particular subjects. Educators use norm-referenced and criterion-referenced tests in evaluating students.

■ **Aptitude tests.** These tests measure your skills and abilities in many specific areas of learning, not your degree of knowledge in specific subjects. The purpose, of course, is to predict how you'll do in school to help you plan a career, or to identify you if you are a gifted student. During your junior or senior year in high school, you must take aptitude tests such as the Scholastic Aptitude Test (SAT). Colleges and universities use them in making admittance decisions.

■ **Entrance exams.** You must take college entrance exams if you want to pursue certain careers. The College Board's Admissions Testing Program (ATP) and the American College Testing Program (ACT) give there tests to would-be college freshmen. The ATP consists of the Scholastic Aptitude Test, a test of standard written English, and 15 optional achievement tests. ACT gives four subjects: English, social studies, mathematics, and natural science. Colleges use both the ATP and the ACT scores for making admission decisions. What is considered a good college admission test score depends on the college considering it, because different colleges have different admission policies in different situations.

A Test Is like a Game

Any test is a game; if you take a standardized test, you're a football quarterback and the test maker is the opposing team: you read the defense, anticipating what kind of defense the opponent has formed and deciding whether to throw the ball to a wide receiver, or to hand it to a runner for a touchdown. If you aren't sure, make a guess.

All the above tests are categorized into two major kinds of examinations in school: the objective or short-answer type, and the subjective or essay type.

Objective Type Tests

The kinds of objective questions or items usually used in the classroom are the alternate-response, multiple-choice, fill-in-the-blanks, and matching.

Alternate-Response Tests

In this type of test you'll select one correct answer from two possible answers, which may be true or false, right or wrong. It seems easy because you're given only two possible answers; it's as if you're asked to select either Donna Rice or Jessica Hahn. Still, be careful in answering the questions because in this type of test, wrong answers are usually subtracted from correct answers. For instance, if you give 11 wrong answers and nine correct answers out of 20 questions, you come up with nothing: 9 minus 11 is less than zero. That's terrible.

True-False Test
Strategies

■ **Tactic 1:** Sentences containing absolutes such as *never, always, all the time,* and *most of the time* are usually *false.*

■ **Tactic 2:** Answer *true* if you're positive that the *thing* being stated is true both in fact and in theory. If you're in doubt about an answer, answer *false.*

■ **Tactic 3:** One word can change an answer so read the sentence word by word and try to analyze what each word means. For instance, be on the lookout for words such as *only, never, always,* and *all.*

Multiple-Choice Tests

Usually the multiple-choice item is presented in two parts: Part I states the problem and Part II gives a series of possible answers marked A, B, and C; A, B, C, and D; or A, B, C, D, and E. Here are some techniques that you can use to attack the questions.

Strategies

■ **Tactic 1:** Answer the sample questions for practice.

■ **Tactic 2:** Answer the easy questions first and the tough questions last.

■ **Tactic 3:** Evaluate the questions and see how they are designed. For example, questions within each test usually progress in difficulty from easy to hard.

■ **Tactic 4:** Watch for subtle word clues such as *a* or *an* rather than *the.*

■ **Tactic 5:** Evaluate whether the longest answer can be the correct one. This is the case in most teacher-made multiple-choice items.

■ **Tactic 6.** Avoid the "loner." If four relatively simple choices appear together and a long or complex fifth choice stands alone, probably the "loner" is not the answer. Example: a) 2, b) 4, c) 8, d) 10, and e) 120. *E* is the loner. (Sometimes, though, the "loner" is the correct answer, so beware!)

■ **Tactic 7:** If you're asked for the *smallest* possible number for something, select the *smallest* or *next to smallest* of the answer choices; when you're asked for the *greatest* number, select the *largest* or the *next to largest* answer. When in doubt, give preference to the *next-to-smallest* and *next-to-largest* choice. Example: a) 20, b) 2, c) 25, d) 17, and e) 15. If asked for the *smallest,* the probable answer is b) 2 or e) 15; if asked for the *greatest* number, the probable answer is c) 25, or a) 20.

■ **Tactic 8:** Search for clues to help you find the right answer. Test makers, for instance, generally use *correct grammar* in the *correct answers* and sometimes use *incorrect grammar* in the *wrong answers* without knowing it, because of their speed in preparing the other answers.

■ **Tactic 9:** If you're sure of a correct answer, select it and don't look for any traps.

■ **Tactic 10:** If you can't figure out the correct answer to a question, pick one. Make a little mark alongside the answer with your pencil and tell yourself, "I shall return!" (That is, if you have the time to do so.)

■ **Tactic 11:** Be on the lookout for non-answers such as *all the above, none of the above, all are true,* and *it cannot be determined from the information given.* Usually they are not the correct answers. If the first three choices are right, for instance, and if the fourth is wrong, and if the fifth is *all of the above,* don't select number 4 or 5. Choose among 1, 2, and 3.

■ **Tactic 12:** Watch out for sentences that contain words such as *all, only, none, never, always, usually,* and *generally.* Often these words are traps; they don't belong to the correct answers. Unless you're sure that it's the right answer, don't select it.

■ **Tactic 13:** Most often, two out of the four or five choices are obvious wrong answers, so eliminate them first. In other words, eliminate the answers which are *clearly* wrong until you come to a point where you are to select between the two *best* choices.

■ **Tactic 14:** Follow your first hunch on a particular answer; don't change it unless you're certain that you're making the right move. In other words, you must follow the rule, "First come, first served."

■ **Tactic 15:** When two answers have *opposite meanings,* usually one of them is the right answer; when two answers express *the same thing,* usually one of the pair is the right answer.

■ **Tactic 16:** Guess if you don't know the answer, but be careful when the test score is calculated by subtracting the wrong answers from the correct answers.

Fill-in-the-Blanks Tests

The fill-in-the-blanks test presents statements with a certain word or words missing. You have to provide the missing "thing" or "things" to complete the sentence. Your answers may be the names of persons, numbers, events, dates, and so on. You cannot use any strategies in answering this type of test. If there's a secret at all, it's recalling the answer from your memory bank; if it's not there, you're in big trouble. Either you have it or you don't. I can't help you. I don't think Vanna White can help you, either. The fill-in-the blanks test requires recalling what you've learned or memorized in the past, so learn the study techniques and the memorization systems in this book!

Matching Tests

In this type of test, you have to match two things, so naturally the test presents two columns: one at the left with blanks where you can put your answers (marked a, b, c, d, etc. or 1, 2, 3, 4, 5, etc.), and one at the right, which can be used as the basis of comparison. You have to select a word or phrase in one column to match one of the answers in the other column. It's like a booth at a state fair, where you have to hold a gun and shoot any of the dolls that are standing in line a few feet from you. The items matched in this kind of test often include events and places, dates and events, books and authors, and inventors and their inventions.

Matching Strategies

■ **Tactic 1:** Start with the right-hand column and work down, matching each answer with the items at the left-hand column.

■ **Tactic 2.** Write the answers you're sure of first and leave the questions you don't know until later.

■ **Tactic 3:** When you've reached the last item of the test, go back to the first question you left unanswered and match it with the prospective answers that have not yet been matched. Use the technique of recalling any and all facts about each item. If you still cannot determine the answer, go to the next unanswered item and match it with the possible remaining answers. Go on and on until you reach the last unanswered question. Then go back again to the first remaining unanswered question and repeat the process until you've answered all the questions.

Essay Type Tests

In the test, you're required not to select answers from several choices but to analyze, interpret, and apply ideas and principles in an organized manner. You'll show your knowledge of the subject matter when you express your own interpretation of the ideas and when you give your reasons for your answers. You'll also describe the relationships of ideas that pertain to persons, things, or events.

One of the secrets to an effective presentation of an essay is to know the key words involved in essay questions. Example: "Discuss the relationship of President Reagan with Khadafy of Libya." *Discuss* is the key word. If you have to *discuss*, you may give details, evidence, advantages, and disadvantages. The answer involves all the six keys to the world of knowledge, *who, what, when, where, why,* and *how,* which are known in the newspaper world as the *five W's* (which include the H.)

Some of the other key words are as follows:

■ **Compare.** Show the similarities and differences between two persons, things, or events. For instance, you can compare the computer with the human brain. You can also compare Imelda Marcos of the Philippines with Michele Duvalier, the former First Lady of Haiti: the size and shape of their hands and feet, the glitter of their jewelry, and the number of pairs of shoes they owned. Comparison involves answers to *hows* and *whys*.

It's like Comparing Imelda Marcos of the Philippines with Michele Duvalier, the Former First Lady of Haiti....

How to Explain

■ **Explain.** Tell in clear details about persons, things, or events: how they were made or how they happened, and why. Explanation requires answers to the five W's and the H, with emphasis on *whys* and *hows*. Examples: Explain how Vietnam was lost.

■ **Describe.** Give an account of something or show what things look alike. A description may tell *who, what, where, how,* or *why*. Example: Describe the reaction of Gary Hart when the news of his relationship with Donna Rice shocked the nation.

■ **Contrast.** Show the differences between persons, things, or events; a contrast, also involves the five W's and the H. Example: Contrast the American and the Russian political systems.

■ **Enumerate.** List a number of things of events in concise form. Enumeration may involve the five W's and the H, but with particular emphasis on *hows* and *whys*. Example: Enumerate the causes of Jim Bakker's rise and fall as a religious leader.

■ **Interpret.** Explain the meaning of something or give your own opinion on things or events. Interpretation seeks answers to *hows* and *whys*. Example: Interpret Patrick Henry's statement: "Give me liberty or give me death."

■ **Summarize.** Discuss briefly the main points of things or events; a summary may involve the use of the five W's and the H. Example: Summarize the causes of the Nicaraguan revolution.

■ **Prove.** Give facts, figures, and reasons to show how or why things happen or can happen. Example: Prove that the October 1987 stock market crash won't be repeated in five years.

■ **Evaluate.** Give the good and bad points and express your own opinion on persons, things, or events. Example: Evaluate the U.S. decision to give aid to the Contras of Nicaragua. (You may ask the help of Oliver North.)

■ **Illustrate.** Explain something by the use of charts, diagrams, and words, which involves the use of *hows* and *whys*.
Example: Illustrate how the circulatory system works.

■ **Trace.** Explain how a person did something or how a thing or event happened or developed. Example: Trace the development of the AIDS epidemic in the United States.

■ **Outline.** Present the main points and secondary points, (usually marked I, II, A, B, 1, 2, 3, and a, b, c), to explain things or events. Outlining involves the use of the five W's and the H. Example: Outline the procedures in writing a book report.

■ **State.** Give the major points about a certain thing or an event, with particular emphasis on the *whats*. Example: State the five main purposes of the US invasion of Grenada.

■ **Relate.** Show how things or events are related to each other, with stress on the *hows* and *whys*. Example: Relate the improvement of the computer to the study of the brain.

■ **Define.** Give the meaning of something, with emphasis on *whats* and *hows*. Example? Define the term, *sexology*.

■ **Justify.** Give facts and figures to prove that an action is right, with weight on the answers to *whys*. Example: Justify Russia's withdrawal of troops from Afghanistan.

Educators use key words or direction words like those described above in essay-type questions. If you analyze these words, you'll see that the test maker merely directs you to do something; if the direction tells you to sit down, don't stand up; if it tells you to stand up, don't sit down. If you know what it wants you to do, you'll do well on essay tests. Just don't forget your friends — *who, what, when, where, why*, and *how* — and you'll be on your way to making high marks on essay tests. Go for it!

Strategies for Tests on Different Subjects 18

When you take a test, it isn't enough to know the subject matter; it isn't enough to memorize the important events. You need to apply some strategies, particularly when you aren't sure of the correct answer. In other words, you must know how to attack the questions.

Generally you can't apply the same strategies to different tests on different subjects. The techniques used in answering vocabulary and spelling questions may be similar in some ways, but they are also different.

In analogies or word relationships, you'll be tested on how well you see relationships between words. In this test you'll apply your knowledge of vocabulary and other subjects.

In most cases you have to read between the lines when you answer reading comprehension tests, picking the main idea from a statement or paragraph. In math you must know first what you are supposed to find out, including the given numbers and the formulas you have to use to solve the problem.

The following pages give the strategies for tests on different subjects.

Vocabulary Test Strategies

(Also see **Multiple-Choice Test Strategies,** page 120.)

You can use various techniques or systems for answering questions on vocabulary or meanings of words tests. Let me discuss them with you one by one:

1. The "It Makes a Difference" System

With this system, you select the answer that looks different from the other four. Let me give you an example: red, white, blue, and green. the most likely answer is *green,* because it's the one that is not in the American flag.

Here's another example:

The letter was *short. Short* means most nearly

A) tall   D) heavy
B) wide   E) dark
C) brief

In the above sample, the words *tall* and *wide* seem to be similar, and the words *heavy* and *dark* also seem to be alike. The word *brief* looks different: it stands alone, so the correct answer is *brief.*

You cannot use the "it makes a difference" system all the time. Sometimes, in fact, it's the opposite case: the correct answer is hidden among the "similar" answers. So beware: like a knife, the "loner" is sometimes double-edged.

2. The Elimination System

In selecting the answer, especially when you don't know the correct one, you must use the so-called "elimination system." Eliminate the wrong choices one by one, starting with the least likely answer, until only one word or phrase is left. It's like Bob Barker announcing five finalists in the *Miss Planet Earth* contest. He starts with the fourth runner-up. When the second runner-up is named, only two contestants remain. When the first runner-up is announced, there's no more choice; the remaining finalist is automatically proclaimed the most beautiful girl in the world!

What? What Do You Mean?

3. The Divide-and-Conquer System

Words are divided into simple words, so study prefixes, suffixes, and roots. (See **Common Prefixes, Suffixes, and Roots,** pages 73-76.) You can dissect words as biology students dissect frogs. When you dissect a frog, it dies, but when you dissect a word, it still lives. *Anthropology,* for instance, can be divided into two roots; *anthropo,* and *logy; anthropo* means man and *logy* means study of; thus *anthropology* means study of man.

4. The Trap Analyzing System

In some instances, test makers intentionally set traps to lure you into selecting a wrong answer. For example, if the question and one of the answers sound alike or look alike, it may be a trap, and most often the answer is wrong.

Strategies for Reading Comprehension Tests

■ **Strategy 1.** Read the questions before you read the passage. By doing that you'll have an idea what the test maker is asking you.

■ **Strategy 2.** If the test maker wants definite factual information, scan the passage, and ask "where are you? where are you?" looking for the fact. If you find it, answer the question and go to the next number.

■ **Strategy 3.** If you read the questions carefully, you'll know what you're looking for, whether the author wants you to gather factual information from the passage or to read between the lines. If you're not good at reading between the lines, first answer the questions that ask for specific facts or information.

Example:

"The secretarial profession is a very old one and has increased in importance with the passage of time. In modern times, the vast expansion of business and industry has greatly increased the need and opportunities for secretaries, and for the first time in history their number has become large."

The quotation best supports the statement that the secretarial profession

A) is older than business and industry
B) demands higher training than it did formerly
C) did not exist in ancient times
D) has greatly increased in size

Find the main idea of the quotation. (See **Main Idea,** page 54.)

Look for key words. The quotation says that the secretarial profession is very old, but it does not say that it is older than business and industry, so *A* is not the correct answer. It does not say that it now demands higher training, so *B* is not the answer. It does not say that it did not exist in ancient times, so *C* is not the answer. As you can see, the word *increased* (the key word) is mentioned twice, and the phrase *has become large* is mentioned once. So *D*, *has greatly increased in size*, is the correct choice.

In choosing the correct answer, look for the main idea or the key words. Be careful though; sometimes the person who prepares the questions will use words in a statement that are also in the quotation. This is done to confuse you so that you may choose it even if it is not the correct answer. In looking for the key words, use your own interpretation. Sometimes the words used in a statement (A, B, or whatever) are not mentioned directly in the quotation. You must interpret what the quotation means or expresses.

Spelling Test Strategies

- **Strategy 1.** Divide the word into syllables and notice how the syllables are spelled. By looking at the word's shape or size, you'll have an idea of whether the spelling is right or wrong.
- **Strategy 2.** Search for the prefixes, suffixes, and roots that may lead you to the correct spelling.
- **Strategy 3.** Look for the double letters, such as double s (ss), double l (ll), double r (rr), or double t (tt) and determine if the spelling is correct. If you have learned the rules on spelling given in this book, you won't have trouble figuring out the correct spelling.
- **Strategy 4.** Write down the word. From the looks of it, you may be able to determine the correct spelling. Sometimes it looks awkward when it is not spelled correctly. If the word is spelled correctly, sometimes it just looks terrific.

Analogies or Word Relationships

These analogy questions will test how well you see relationships between words and apply those relationships to other words. To do well on the analogy questions, you should have a good vocabulary and knowledge of subjects such as history and science.

Strategies

■ **Strategy 1: One-by-one elimination.** You must eliminate one by one all obviously wrong answers until you are left with the best answer to the question. As you know, all the answers are possible, but only one is the correct answer.

■ **Strategy 2: Word comparison.** Determine how the first word is related to the second word. Then select the word that is related to the third word in the same way as the first and second words are related.

Kinds of Relationships

1. Synonyms. In this relationship the words are the same or close in meaning. Examples: pretty and attractive, kind and affectionate, E. T.'s and Cocoons.

Example:

DISHONOR is to DISGRACE as WISDOM is to

A) skill   C) endowment
B) discipline   D) knowledge

Explanation: DISHONOR is similar to DISGRACE in meaning, and WISDOM indicates KNOWLEDGE; therefore, *D* is the correct answer.

2. Antonyms. In this relationship, the two words are opposites, such as tall and short, weak and strong, fat and thin.

Example:

NIGHT is to DAY as EAST is to

A) north   C) south
B) west   D) northeast

Explanation: NIGHT is the opposite of DAY and EAST is the opposite of WEST, so *B* is the correct answer.

3. Part relationship. One word stands for the part of a group or class, and the other word stands for the group or class.

Example:

TIGER is to CAT as GRAPEFRUIT is to

A) eggplant   C) vegetable
B) citrus   D) legumes

Explanation: TIGER is part of the CAT family and GRAPEFRUIT is part of the CITRUS fruit family, so *B* is the correct answer.

4. Cause-and-effect relationship. In this analogy, one word in a pair produces an effect, which is represented by the other word in the pair.

Example:

PRACTICE is to SUCCESS as STUDY is to

A) learning   C) laziness
B) boredom   D) dumbness

Explanation: You can be a SUCCESS as an athlete (or whatever) if you do a lot of PRACTICE. LEARNING can be easy if you STUDY efficiently.

5. Purpose relationship. In this analogy, one word is an object and the other word gives the purpose of the object.

Example:

THERMOMETER is to TEMPERATURE as COMPASS is to

A) distance   C) direction
B) wind   D) mile

Explanation: A THERMOMETER is used to find the TEMPERATURE and a COMPASS is used to show the DIRECTION, so *C* is the correct answer.

6. Object-action relationship. One word in the pair is the object or the result of an action, which is represented by the other word in the pair.

Example:

WATER is to SPILL as ICE is to

A) rain   C) run
B) slip   D) play

Explanation: You can SPILL water if you're not careful. On any cold, snowy day, you can SLIP on ice while walking, if you don't watch out. So *B* is the correct answer.

7. Identification relationship. A person or a thing is closely identified with another person or thing. When you see or hear something, you think of the "other" person or thing. They are like Cagney and Lacey.

Example:

POLICEMAN is to GUN as FIREMAN is to

A) stethoscope   C) hose
B) shovel   D) broom

Explanation: A uniformed man with a GUN can be recognized immediately as a POLICEMAN because he carries the weapon that he uses to fight crime. A uniformed man with a big HOSE can be recognized immediately as a FIREMAN because he has the tool that he uses to fight fire, so C is the correct answer.

Strategies for Solving Mathematics Problems

You can find the answers to math problems, no matter how complicated they are, by addition, subtraction, multiplication, and division, or by conversion of millimeters to centimeters, ounces to pounds, fractions into decimals, and so on. First, though, you must know whether to add or subtract, multiply or divide; it's like knowing whether you're going east or west. If you don't know, you're lost.

■ **Strategy 1.** The first time you're faced with a math problem, figure out how you're going to solve it. You must know the following:

- What you are supposed to find out.
- The given numbers.
- The principles or formulas needed to solve the problem

■ **Strategy 2.** Write the numbers carefully. Be extra careful in writing 0, 6 or 8, and vice versa. Don't write a 3 that looks like a 5 or a 1 that looks like a 7, or vice versa. The columns should be in straight lines, so that you don't make mistakes in addition or subtraction.

■ **Strategy 3.** Be sure to check the units of measure. If they are not in the proper units convert them into the correct units, such as millimeters into centimeters, ounces into pounds, or kilometers into miles. Don't try to add pounds to ounces, for example.

■ **Strategy 4.** Use diagrams, as much as possible, such as squares, triangles, and other shapes. Label all the given numbers if such diagrams are needed to simplify solving.

■ **Strategy 5.** In solving any problem, particularly in a multiple-choice math test, don't glance at the choices (A, B, C, D, E) before you work on the problem. Work on the problem first, and when you have an answer, see if it matches any of the given answers. It's like comparing your numbers with the numbers in a lotto; if your numbers don't match the winning numbers, you didn't win and you must try another time. So if your answer is not among the choices, it's not the correct answer. Try again to solve it.

■ **Strategy 6.** If you don't really know how to solve the problem, you'd better guess; that's better than leaving the question unanswered. Use the following elimination system:

- First eliminate the least probable answers.
- Eliminate the lowest and highest values among the remaining answers.
- Then select the most likely answer from the answers that remain.

Math Test Techniques

Thomas F. Ewald, a former college instructor, (see Page 88), gives the following advice on multiplication problems:

Solve the following multiplication problem:

3453 × 4376 =

A) 15,112,432   C) 15,110,328
B) 15,121,324   D) 15,432,222

How long did it take you? If it took more than five seconds, you need this technique!

Take the last digit of each of the numbers to be multiplied against each other; now find the product of these two digits (that is, multiply them against each other): $3 \times 6 = 18$. Now notice the last digit of the correct answer above, Answer C. (You did get the right answer, didn't you?) It's 8. What was the last digit of the simple problem we just did (3×6)? That was also 8. It's not a coincidence. It will happen every time! As long as only one answer is given with the correct last digit, it's easy to pick the right answer! ʹ

If more than one answer ends in the correct digit, you'll have to do the actual multiplication. Also, my advice won't work if "none of the above" is given as an option. But it will help some of the time and can save precious seconds, or even minutes.

On some tests, such as the SAT, speed is extra important. Tactics like the one above helped me achieve a perfect score on the math portion of the SAT! It can be done!

Other Uses of the Technique

I tried Ewald's technique and it worked. I found out that you can also use this technique in solving *addition, subtraction,* and *division* problems.

For example, you are asked to add the following numbers:

$$388$$
$$359$$
$$159$$
$$312$$
$$746$$
$$324$$

A) 3727   C) 1789
B) 2288   D) 4725

In solving addition problems, (see also pages 81-84), add the last digits of the numbers. In the above example, $8 + 9 + 9 + 2 + 6 + 4 = 38$. Now stop adding, and take the last digit of the answer (which is 8). Compare it with the last digits of the answers given as choices. In this case, *B* is the correct answer because 2288 ends with the number 8. Follow the same rule with subtraction. Take the last digit of the answer (subtract only the last digits, for example, $9 - 4 = 5$) and compare it with the last digits of the answers given as choices.

In division, however, the number that is to be chosen as the correct answer is the *first* digit of your answer, not the *last*. As soon as you get the *first* digit of the answers, stop dividing and compare that digit with the *first* digits of the four answers given as choices. If it is the same *first* digit of any of the choices, that choice is the *answer!* If there are at least two choices with the same first digits, continue solving until you get two digits, and so on.

If "none of the above" is among the choices, you can select it if the last digit of your answer doesn't match the last digit of any of the answers given as choices in *multiplication, addition,* and *subtraction.* If *"none of the above"* option is given in a *division* problem, pick it if the first digit of your answer doesn't match the first digits of any of the answers given as choices.

Hints for Solving Physics Problems and Related Word Problems in Mathematics

Dr. Sherman P. Kanagy, II, a professor of math and physics at Purdue University in Westville, Indiana, gives the following tips for solving physics and math problems:

- Write down what is given, translated into mathematical form. For example, "the acceleration was 4 m/s^2" becomes "a = 4 m/s^2." Be very careful to translate every phase.
- When possible, draw a picture or diagram that enables you to visualize the situation of the problem. Be sure to represent accurately what the problem says.
- Write down the unknown in algebraic form: v = ? This step makes clear what your goal is in solving the problem.
- Identify the equation that relates the unknown quantity to the known quantities. Solve for the unknown. Note that if the unknown quantity is the ratio of two other quantities, you do not necessarily have to find the two other quantities separately.
- Insert the actual numbers as late as possible. Carry out the algebra as far as you can, until the unknown is alone on one side of the equation and all the known quantities are on the other side. THEN put in the numbers. The fewer "intermediate" quantities you calculate numerically, the less is your chance of making an error.
- Always state explicitly the meaning of the number you get as an answer. If you are solving for velocity, your answer should take the form v = 15.25 m/s rather than simply 15.25. Be sure to include the appropriate units with the answer.
- Do not skip steps. Write everything down, including the simplest algebraic operation.

Number Series Exams

The Number/Letter Puzzle Exam

In this kind of exam, a set of five suggested answers is given for each group of questions that appears below. Don't try to memorize these answers because each test has different sets.

To answer each question, find which of the suggested answers appear in the question. These numbers and letters may be in any order.

1. 0 Q M 1 I V 6 7

2. V 1 9 B 8 N 5 M

3. B 9 I M 5 1 0 Q

A = 9, 1, I, M
B = 0, 1, V, B
C = 8, 9, M, B
D = 7, 0, I, V

This type of question is not only confusing; it's also time-consuming. In answering it, you must first compare the numbers and letters contained in the suggested answers (first "A," and then "B," and so on. In answering question number 1, for instance, you don't find 9 (from possible answer A) in the question, so forget 1, I, and M and go straight to answer "B." 0, 1, I, and V are in the question, but B isn't, so proceed to "C." The 8 isn't there, so don't continue any longer but go to "D"; 7, 0, I, and V are in the question. That's it! D is the correct answer.

This type of question is used in several exams, particularly in several civil service exams.

Number or Letter Series Test Problems

These tests, which are considered nonverbal, are given to measure your ability to find the "missing link."

Here are some strategies:

Strategy 1: Find the rule that creates the series of numbers or letters.

Strategy 2: Find out which number or letter comes next or is missing.

Strategy 3: Find the patterns used.

In the number series, you'll discover that the pattern or relation-ship may involve the use of any of the following:

- addition
- subtraction
- multiplication
- division
- squaring
- cubing
- square roots
- cube roots.

Simple Number Series. Each of the three sample questions below gives a series of seven numbers. Each number follows a certain pattern or order. Choose what will be the next one or two numbers in that series if the pattern is continued.

---

1. 6   8   10   12   14   16   18   ....

    A) 22   C) 24
    B) 20   D) 21
                                   E) 23

In this question, the pattern is to add 2 to each number: 6 + 2 = 8; 8 + 2 = 10; 10 + 2 = 12; 12 + 2 = 14; 14 + 2 = 16; 16 + 2 = 18. The next number in the series is 18 + 2 which equals 20. B is the correct answer. Here's how it's done:

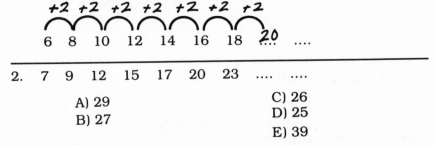

---

2. 7   9   12   15   17   20   23   ....

    A) 29   C) 26
    B) 27   D) 25
                                   E) 39

In this question, the pattern is to add 2 to the first number (7 + 2 = 9); add 3 to the second number (9 + 3 = 12; add 3 to the third number (12 + 3 = 15); add 2 to the fourth number (15 + 2 = 17); add 3 to the fifth number (17 + 3 = 20); add 3 to the sixth number

(20 + 3 = 23). To continue the series, add 2 to the next number (23 + 2 = 25). D is the correct answer. Here's how it's done:

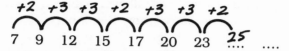

As you can see, the order or pattern is to add 2 once, then add 3 twice. Get it?

---

3.   9   10   8   9   7   8   6   ....

        A) 7   C) 9

        B) 5   D) 8

                                        E) 6

In this question, the pattern is to add 1 to the first number, subtract 2 from the next, add 1, subtract 2, and so on. (9 + 1 = 10; 10 − 2 = 8; 8 + 1 = 9; 9 − 2 = 7; 7 + 1 = 8; 8 − 2 = 6; 6 + 1 = 7). Thus A is the correct answer. Here's how it's done:

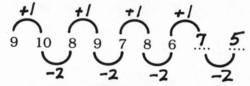

Complex Number Series. These questions are more difficult and the correct answer must be chosen from sets of two numbers. Your job is to select the correct set of two numbers.

The technique used in this type of question is to compare the first number to the third number, the second to the fourth, the third to the fifth, and so on. To make it easier, draw lines to join the numbers as you analyze the pattern. So that you won't be confused, draw the lines both above and below the numbers. (When you finish answering the questions, you may erase these lines on the question or answer sheet.) It's as simple as connecting Monday to Wednesday, Wednesday to Friday, Tuesday to Thursday, and Thursday to Saturday. Then all you have to do is find the pattern within each group of numbers.

---

1.   7   13   8   15   10   17   13   19   17   ....

        A) 23 24   C) 25 26

        B) 21 22   D) 27 28

                                    E) 29 30

There are two patterns in this series. Add 2 to the second, fourth, sixth, and the eighth numbers and add to the first, third, fifth, seventh, and ninth numbers as follows: + 1, + 2, + 3, + 4, + 5. B is the correct answer. Here's how it's done:

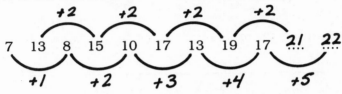

---

2. 1   7   2   6   4   5   7   4   ....

A) 13 3   C) 11 3
B) 15 2   D) 17 2
                 E) 12 2

For the first, third, fifth, and seventh numbers, you have to add 1, add 2, add 3, and add 4. For the second, fourth, sixth, and eigth numbers, subtract 1 each time. C is the correct answer. Here's how it's done:

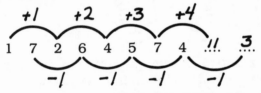

Letter Series. In this kind of problem, too, you will look for the pattern or order. Take this example.

a   d   g   j   m   p   —

If numbers had been used in this series, it would be easier to get the answer, but by using your fingers, you'll find easily that the letters advance by three places in the alphabet. That's the pattern, and the correct answer is *s*.

Letters in groups. These groups may be pairs of letters. Let's take this example:

c a   f m   p q   p q   f m   —

As you can see, the p q is repeated, and then the f m comes again, so you have to go back again to c a. That's the pattern, and the correct answer is c a.

Part III

The Basics of Grammar
The Basics of Writing
Using the Internet to Improve Grades
How to Think Effectively
7-Point Formula to Be an Honor Student
Brief Summary and More Strategies

The Basics of Grammar

It's a fact: To be proficient in speaking and writing, you should master and practice grammar and word usage whether you are in the intermediate grades, in high school or in college. With a well-rounded knowledge of writing concepts and processes, you'll be able to give facts and express your opinion with clarity, variety, and style.

You must be proficient in writing a sentence: combining a subject and a verb to express a complete thought. Moreover, you should be able to combine two sentences into one by using the so-called coordination conjunctions, such as *and, or, either...or,* and others.

This chapter discusses sentence structure.

I. The Sentence Structure

This section discusses a group of words, a single word, the kinds of sentences, the parts of a sentence, the main sentence forms, the types of sentences, and the paragraphs.

A. **A Group of Words**. A sentence is a group of words consisting of a subject and a verb and expressing a complete thought. Examples:

- The **world** is round.
(**World** is the subject and **is** is the verb.)
- **John went** to school.
(**John** is the subject and **went** is the verb.)

Sometimes, a single word or verb can also be a sentence if it expresses a complete thought. This is usually done by professional writers.

Example: Concentrate. (It is understood that a *you* precedes concentrate.)

B. **The Kinds of Sentences.** The four kinds of sentences are *declarative, interrogative, imperative,* and *exclamatory.*

1. **Declarative Sentence.** A telling statement, a *declarative sentence* ends with a period.

Example: Gorbachev has a map on his head.

2. **Interrogative Sentence.** Asking a question, an *interrogative sentence* ends with a question mark.

Example: In what part of Israel did the Scud land?

3. **Imperative Sentence.** A statement giving a command or making a request, an *imperative sentence* ends with a period.

Example: You go to school today.

4. **Exclamatory Sentence.** Telling excitement or surprise, an *exclamatory sentence* ends with an exclamation mark.

Example: The marathoners are coming!

The Marathoners Are Coming!

C. **The Parts of a Sentence.** A sentence consists of a subject and a verb. The subject, usually placed before the verb, is the person or thing spoken or written about which may answer the question *Who?* or *What?* The verb, which may consist of a word or a group of words, shows the subject's action or state of being. However, the part of the sentence that tells something about the subject, which may include an action verb or a linking verb, is commonly called a *predicate.*

Examples:

■ The **wind** *is* cold.

(**Wind** is the subject that answers the question of *what?* and **is** is the verb. The word group **is cold** is called the predicate.

■ The **player** hits the ball.

(**Player** is the subject and **hits** is the verb. The word group **hits the ball** is called the predicate.)

D. **The Main Sentence Forms.** The main sentence forms are (1) the *word,* the major sentence structure which serves as a part of speech; (2) the *phrase,* which represents a group of words; and (3) the *clause,* which also represents a group of words. We will discuss the phrase and the clause.

1. **Phrases.** Not containing a subject-verb combination, a *phrase* is a group of two or more words serving as a part of the sentence. The main types of phrases are:

a. Verb phrase

b. Gerund phrase

c. Participial phrase

d. Prepositional phrase

e. Infinitive phrase

Example of a phrase: The athlete **is running.**

(Here, **is running** is the phrase.)

(Note: For definitions and examples of the above phrases, see Chapter 20.)

2. **Clauses.** A *clause* is a group of two or more words containing a subject-verb combination, usually forming part of a compound or complex sentence The main types of clauses follow:

a. *Independent Clause.* An independent clause is a group of two or more words that expresses a complete thought.

Example: **Johnny rides the bicycle,** and **his sister plays the piano.**

b. *Dependent Clause.* A dependent clause is a group of two or more words that expresses an incomplete thought.

Example: **After she finished the job,** she left to see a movie.

The bold-type group of words comprises the dependent clause.

E. **Types of Sentences.** The independent and dependent clauses combine to form various types of sentences, such as simple, compound, complex, and compound-complex sentences.

1. **Simple Sentence.** A *simple sentence,* which has an independent clause, makes a single statement. It has a subject-verb combination.

Example:

■ Charles flies a kite.

2. **Compound Sentence.** A *compound sentence* is a sentence containing two or more independent coordinate clauses.

Examples:

■ He drives the station wagon, but he prefers the Mustang.
■ Linda works during the day, and her husband goes to school at night.

3. **Complex Sentence.** A *complex sentence* is a sentence composed of one or more dependent clauses.

Example:

■ He waters his grandparents' plants **whenever he goes to their house.**

The **bold-type** group of words comprises a dependent clause.

4. **Compound-Complex Sentence.** Having two or more independent clauses serving as modifiers, the *compound-complex sentence* has two or more subject-verb combinations. It has also one or more different clauses serving as modifiers.

F. **The Paragraphs.** A paragraph is a group of sentences with a single thought. It has a topic sentence that expresses the main idea.

II. The Parts of Speech

Grammar is the science of studying and analyzing the functions of words in a sentence. These sentence functions are generally known as the parts of speech, which are *noun, pronoun, verb, adjective, adverb, preposition, conjunction,* and *interjection.*

A. **Nouns.** A noun names or identifies a person, a place, a thing, an idea, a quality, etc., (man, book, bomb).

1. *Proper Noun.* A proper noun is the name of a person or a thing (Schwarzkopf, Cuba, Buick). It is always capitalized

whether at the beginning or in any other parts of a sentence.

2 *Common Noun.* A common noun is any one of a class of persons, places, or things (soldier, desert, jet). Unless placed at the beginning of a sentence, a common noun does not begin with a capital letter.

3. *Collective Noun.* A collective noun is the name of a group of persons or things (squad, division, branch).

B. **Pronouns.** A pronoun is any one of the class of signal words that assumes the place of a noun.

Examples:

My (mine), your (yours), his (his), her (hers), its (its), our (ours), and their (theirs).

Myself, yourself, himself, herself, itself, ourselves, yourselves, and themselves.

When, whom, whose, that, and which.

C. **Verbs.** A verb expresses action, occurrence, or state of being (is/was, are/were, goes/went, play/played).

D. **Adjectives.** An adjective is a modifier that describes a noun or a pronoun (big, wide, beautiful).

E. **Adverbs**. An adverb is a modifier that describes a verb, another adverb, an adjective, a phrase, or a clause (when, then, slowly).

F. **Propositions.** A preposition is a relation or function word that connects a noun or a pronoun to another element of the sentence (in, to, of, for).

G. **Conjunctions.** A conjunction is a word or a group of words that connects words, phrases, clauses, or sentences (and, or, but, either...or, not only...but also).

H. **Interjections.** An interjection is an exclamatory word inserted into an utterance (Wow! What a beautiful dress!)

III. The Verbs

A. **Kinds of Verbs.** The two major kinds of verbs are the regular verbs and the irregular verbs. Regular verbs are those verbs whose past tense can be formed by adding **ed** (talk/talk**ed**). Irregular verbs cannot add **ed** to past tense (speak/spo**ke**).

1. **Regular Verbs**

Examples of regular verbs

Infinitive
to launch
to advance

Present
launches
advances

Past
launched
advanced

Past participle
had launched
had advanced

As you'll notice in regular verbs, the past tense and the past participle are the same.

2. **Irregular Verbs**

Examples of irregular verbs

Infinitive
to drive
to know

Present
drives
knows

Past
drove
knew

Past Participle
had driven
had known

In irregular verbs, the past tense and the past participle are the same.

The irregular verb *to be* contains the verbs *is, am, are, was, were, be, being,* and *been.*

3. **Linking Verbs**. A linking verb is a verb that doesn't show action. Its job is to link the subject with a noun, a pronoun, or an adjective.

Examples:

■ My wife **is** a doctor.

■ Karla **looked** pale after her speech before the class.

4. **Transitive Verbs.** A *transitive verb* is a verb that needs a direct object to complete its meaning.

Example of a transitive verb:

■　He **blew** the **horn**.

In the example, **blew** is the transitive verb and **horn** is the direct object.

5. **Intransitive Verbs.** An *intransitive verb* is a verb that does not need an object to complete its meaning.

Example of an intransitive verb:

■ The students **are** coming.

In the example, *are,* a verb of *to be,* is intransitive; it doesn't need a direct object to complete its meaning.

B. **Verb Voices.** A verb has two voices: *active* and *passive.* A verb in the active voice is a verb whose subject does something while a verb in the passive voice is a verb whose subject gets the action.

Example of active voice:

■ An Egyptian soldier killed two Iraquis.

Example of passive voice:
■ Two Iraquis were killed by an Egyptian soldier.

As you can see, the above sentence was inverted to change the voice from active to passive. In the first example, the subject does something, while in the second example, the subject receives the action.

C. **Verb Parts.** The three major parts of a verb are the *present*, the *past*, and the *past participle*. To form the past and the past participles in regular verbs, we have to add *d, ed,* or *t* to the present form. (Sometimes, however, the fourth part of a verb is called a *present participle*.)

Present
walk
negotiate
spend

Past
walked
negotiated
spent

Past Participle
had walked
had negotiated
had spent

Present participle
walking
negotiating
spending

D. **Subject-Verb Agreement**. The most common errors among students in English composition pertain to the subject-verb agreement. The rule dictates that if the subject is *singular,* the verb must be *singular,* and if the *subject is plural,* the verb must be *plural,* too. This is done in both regular and irregular verbs.

Examples:

- He **walks** slowly
- The U.S. commander **meets** the Egyptian general in the Sahara desert.

In the above regular (**walks**) and irregular (**meets**) verbs, we add *s* to form the present tense.

However, in some irregular verbs, *es,* not merely **s,** is added to the verb to form the present tense for singular subjects.

Example: Michael punch**es** his rival on the nose.

Furthermore, it is understood that if the subject is plural, the verb must be in plural form; it doesn't need the addition of *s* or *es*.

Examples:

- The athletes **meet** in the gym every day.
- Peter and his group **attend** an evening class.

E. **Verb Tenses.** The verb tenses discussed in this subsection are present, past, future, present perfect, past perfect, future perfect, present progressive, past progressive, and future progressive.

1. **Present, Past, and Future Tenses**

a. *Present Tense.* The present tense of a verb shows action that is happening at the present time (now or today).

Example:

■ Some people view paintings at the museum.

b. *Past Tense.* The past tense of a verb shows action that happened in the past.
Example:

■ Whitney Houston **sang** the *Star Spangled Banner* during a Super Bowl.

c. *Future Tense.* The future tense of a verb shows action that is going to happen (this afternoon, tomorrow, or any other day to come).
Example:

■ Madonna **will get married** soon.

Recapitulation: Here are more examples:
Present tense: eat/eats, bark/barks
Past tense: ate, barked
Future tense: will eat, will bark

2. **Present Perfect, Past Perfect, and Future Perfect Tenses**

a. *Present Perfect Tense.* The present perfect tense of a verb shows action that has been completed by the present time, but without stating any specific time.

Example:

■ The hunters **have come** home from the mountains.

b. *Past Perfect Tense.* The past perfect tense of a verb shows action that had been completed during a definite period in the past before another happening.
Example:

■ We **had flown** three hours before we knew that one of our companions was not on the plane.

c. *Future Perfect Tense.* The future perfect tense of a verb shows action that will have been completed anytime in the future.
Example:

■ Catherine **will have been graduated** from college by the time she reaches 25.

Recapitulation: Here are more examples:

Present Perfect: has, have
Past Perfect: had
Future Perfect: will have, shall have, will have been, shall have been

3. **Present Progressive, Past Progressive, and Future Progressive Tenses.**
a. *Present Progressive Tense.* The present progressive tense shows action at the present time, using the *to be* verbs *is, am,* or *are* with the present participle.
Example:

■ President Clinton **is reading** the book *I've Gone to the Persian Gulf* by Dan Quayle.

(In this example, **is** is the verb and **reading** is the present participle; hence **is reading** expresses the present progressive tense.)

b. *Past Progressive Tense.* The past progressive tense shows action in the past using the *to be* verb *was* or *were* with the present participle.
Example:

■ My girlfriend **was doing** her homework when I came.

c. *Future Progressive Tense.* The future progressive tense shows action in the future using the *to be* verbs *will be* or *shall be* with the present participle.
Example:

■ They **will be meeting** in the classroom tomorrow.

Recapitulation: Here are more examples:
Present Progressive: am writing, is writing, are writing
Past Progressive: was writing, were writing
Future Progressive: will be writing, shall be writing

IV. The Rules of Capitalization

Here are some rules on capitalization:
1. Capitalize the first letter of the first word in each sentence.
2. Capitalize the word I.
3. Capitalize the first letter of all proper names of persons (Noriega, Khadafy, Baker).
4. Capitalize the first letter of the days of the week, the months of the year, and any special days (Monday, January, New Year's).
5. Capitalize the first letter of all other proper nouns, such as cities, states, countries, rivers, and mountains (Farmington Hills, New York, Mississippi River).
6. Capitalize the first word, the last word, and all important words in any title, except the words *a, an, of, the, and, but, or,* and *nor,* and other prepositions with four or less letters, except when placed as the first word of a title (*For Dreams Must Die, The Making of an Honor Student.*)
7. Capitalize the titles of people (Dr., Mr., Mrs.)
8. Capitalize the names of languages and religions (English, Roman Catholic).

9. Capitalize the names of significant events (The Day the Earth Stood Still).

11. Capitalize the first letter of all words used in the greeting and the first word in the closing of a letter (Dear Laura, Lovingly yours).

12. Capitalize the names of companies and organizations (Johnson Painting Company, Madonna Fan Club).

13. Capitalize the first word of a direct quotation ("Read my lips; there will be no new taxes," President Bush said)

V. The Uses of Punctuation Marks

The following are some rules on punctuation:

1. Use a period at the end of every declarative (statement) and imperative (command) sentence.

Example:

Statement: Brook Shields doesn't want to marry a prince.
Command: Go to the reunion, now!

2. Use a period after initials and abbreviations (M., V., S., Lt., Capt.).

3. Use a comma to separate the day and the year (February 14, 1991); to separate the city and the state (Detroit, Michigan); and to separate words or phrases in a series (actors, singers, and dancers).

4. Use a comma before and after an appositive to separate it from the rest of the sentence (Arthur, the valedictorian of the class, will take up medicine in college).

5. Use a comma between two parts of a short compound sentence if punctuation is needed for clarity (I have been courting her for the past several years, and I am happy that she has decided to marry me).

6. Use a question mark to end every sentence asking a question (Where are you?).

7. Use an exclamation mark at the end of an exclamatory word or sentence (Oh No! You should not have done that!).

8. Use an apostrophe to shorten a word or a phrase (you are—you're; who is—who's).

9. Use an apostrophe and an *s* to show ownership of a noun

(city's water system). When a word ends with an *s,* put an apostrophe after the *s* to show possession (Jones' car).

10. Use quotation marks at the beginning and the end of direct quotations ("Come and get me!" the kidnapers barked.).

11. Use a semicolon to separate two closely related main clauses in the absence of a conjunction, such as *and* (Terry will go to the movie; his friends will see the football game.).

12. Use a semicolon to separate clauses joined by such words as *however, hence,* and *therefore* (He didn't pass the entrance exam; hence, he can't go to college this fall.).

13. Use a semicolon to separate enumerated items if they are long or have too many commas.

Example:

> The candidate for the position must have the ability to use mechanical, electrical, and electronic test equipment; to provide technical supervision and guidance to supervisors and technicians; and to plan and coordinate alteration, maintenance, and repair activities with contractors, managers, and maintenance and operations supervisors.

14. Use a colon at the end of a formal greeting in a letter. (Dear Sir: Dear Madam: Dear Gentlemen:).

15. Use a colon to introduce a list (The recipe must include the following: 1 cup sugar, 2 cups lemonade, 2 pieces bread, and 5 slices meat.)

16. Use a hyphen to separate compound words. Use a hyphen if the pair of words forms an adjective that is placed before the noun. (Well-known author, first-class service.)

17. Use a hyphen for fractions serving as adjectives. (A two-thirds can of coke.)

18. Use dashes instead of parentheses (In case you go to the picnic—if you would really like to meet me—bring samples of your writings.).

19. Use dashes to separate an "aside" from the rest of the sentence. (At the class reunion—people coming from different parts of the country—Peter and Joann, former high school sweethearts, met for the first time after not seeing each other for 20 years.)

20. Use parentheses to enclose additional material that would interrupt the flow of the sentence. (As he talked with

Elizabeth (after learning that she is still single), Ronald expressed his interest in seeing her again.).

21. If what is inside the parentheses is a complete sentence, put a period at the end of the sentence. (See **Writing,** Chapter 20 of this book.).

VI. The Idiom

An idiom is an expression whose meaning is not predictable from the standard meanings of its constituents as *beating around the bush.* An idiom usually involves the combination of two things, for example, a noun or verb with a proposition.

Examples:

afflicted with: She is *afflicted with* pneumonia.

argue with: I don't with to *argue with* you.

comply with: You must *comply with* the regulations of the university.

according to: *According to* our teacher, we should also consult our textbook to write a complete report on what we talked about yesterday.

prior to: *Prior to* his election to the governorship, he was a city mayor.

decide on: I'll *decide on* the matter tomorrow.

decide to: He'll *decide to* solve the conflict.

20

The Basics of Writing

In this chapter, we seek to find ways on how to write with clarity, coherence, and effectiveness. That is, you have to find ways on how to be a good writer, whether you write a sentence, a paragraph, an essay, a report, or a story.

I. Writing

In chapter 19, we discussed the *phrase* (a group of two or more words without a subject-verb combination that forms a part of a sentence) and the *clause* (a group of two or more words containing a subject-verb combination that usually forms a part of a compound or complex sentence).

The different kinds of phrases and their definitions are as follows:

A. **The Verb Phrase.** A *verb phrase* is a group of two or more words containing a helping verb and a main verb.
Example:
■ Catherine **is willing** to go to the movie theater.

In this example, **is** is the auxiliary or helping verb and **willing** is the main verb. Therefore, **is willing** is the verb phrase.

More examples:

Helping Verb

must
has been
will be

Main Verb
write
writing
writing

Verb Phrase
must write
has been writing
will be writing

Here's a list of the most commonly used helping verbs:

is
am
are
was
were
be
been
being
has
have
had
do
did
done
must
can
could
may
might
will
shall
should
would

Generally, in a declarative sentence, the verb phrase is grouped together.

Example:

■ Baghdad should have been invaded by the allied troops to force Saddam Hussein to surrender.

In this example, **should have been invaded** is the verb phrase.

However, in an interrogative sentence, the verb phrase is usually separated.

Example:
■ **Have** you **been disappointed** in love?

B. **Gerund Phrase.** A *gerund phrase* is a group of words containing a gerund and any related modifiers and other elements of the sentence. A *gerund* is a verbal noun that tells an action and ends in *ing.*

(Note: A *gerund phrase* is one of the three so-called *verbal phrases*: the others are the *participial phrase* and the *infinitive phrase*. A *verbal* is a word derived from a verb that usually serves in a sentence as a noun, an adjective, or an adverb.)

Examples of a gerund phrase used as a noun:

■ **Thinking** is a good habit.

In this example, **thinking** is the gerund.

■ **His helping** others makes him a kind man.

In this example, **helping** is the gerund and **his helping** is the gerund phrase.

C. **Participial Phrase.** One of the verbal phrases, a *participial phrase* is a group of words containing a participle and any other modifiers and other elements of the sentence. (Note: A *participle* is a major part of a verb, which may be called the *present participle* or the *past participle.*)

Regular Tense

Talk
walk
look

Present
Participle

talking
walking
looking

Past Tense

talked
walked
looked

Past Participle

had talked
had walked
had looked

1. *Introductory Participial Phrase.* When the phrase is at the beginning of a sentence, it's called an *introductory participial phrase.* It maybe composed of one or more words, with a comma after the phrase.

Examples:
- **Smiling,** Catherine walked onto the stage and made a speech.
- **Looking happy,** Denise accepted her achievement award from the school principal.

2. *Participial Phrase Used As an Adjective.* When used as an adjective, a participial phrase can be placed following the noun or the pronoun it modifies.

Example:
- Two dogs, **walking on the grass,** barked at the letter carrier.

In this example, **walking on the grass,** placed after the subject, is the participial phrase used as an adjective.

3. *Past Participial Phrase.* Another type of a participial phrase is the one that has a past participle. To make a past participle, we add *ed* to a regular verb with the aid of the so-called helping verbs such as *have, has,* and *had.*

Examples:

Infinitive
to melt
to finish

Past
melted
finished

Past Participle
had melted
had finished

- The ice on the pavement **had melted** when Peter arrived.
- He **had finished** reading when his friend telephoned him.

However, in using irregular verbs, as learned in the previous chapter, we can't add *ed* to make the past participle.

Examples:

Infinitive
to fly
to grow

Past
flew
grew

Past Participle
had flown
had grown

- The bird **had flown** when the rains fell.
- The grass **had grown** so tall that he decided to cut it.

a. *Describing a Noun.* A *past participle* is also used to describe a noun. When used as an adjective, the verb form is called a verbal.

Example:
- A **damaged** book was returned to the library

b. *Beginning a Sentence.* A past participle may also be used at the beginning of a sentence.

Example:
- **Saddened** by the death of his father, the son stopped studying.

c. *Using somewhere, somehow.* We can also place somewhere or somehow in a sentence any participial phrase with a past participle.

Example:
- The bomb, **dropped** on the enemy position, did not explode.

4. **Infinitive Phrase.** The *infinitive phrase* is a group of words containing an infinitive and any related modifiers and other elements of the sentence. (Note: An infinitive is a verb form usually containing the word *to* and a verb.)

Examples:
- to meet: He canceled his trip abroad **to meet his girlfriend** in the city.
- to finish: **To finish his writing,** she did an extensive research work.

In this example, **To finish his writing** is an infinitive phrase placed before the subject *she.*

5. **Prepositional Phrase.** A *prepositional phrase* is a group of words beginning with a preposition and ending with a noun or a proper noun.

Examples:
- He went **to the farm**.
- **Below the table** are some books.

The prepositional phrases are **to the farm** and **Below the table.**

(Note: The noun or the pronoun is the object of the preposition.)

D. Types of Clauses. As discussed in chapter 19, the major types of clauses are the independent and dependent clauses. (An independent clause is a group of two or more words that expresses a complete thought, while a dependent clause is a group of two or more words that expresses an incomplete thought.)

1. **Noun Clause.** A *noun clause* is a dependent clause that serves as a noun in a sentence. It usually begins with such words as:

who, which, what
that, those
when, where
whatever, whichever, whoever

Examples:
- I know **that you are sad.**
- **What you have explained** is enough.

2. **Adjective Clause.** An *adjective clause* is a dependent clause which serves as an adjective in a sentence. It usually begins with such words as:
which, that
when, where
who, whom, whose

Example:
- The woman **who looks like** Elizabeth Taylor is Lebanese.

3. **Adverb Clause.** An *adverb clause* is a dependent clause which serves as an adverb in a sentence. It usually begins with words that answer the questions:
When? Where?
How? Why? How much?

When? Where?

It may also have beginning words such as the following:
then, when
while, where
after, since, so that
because, inasmuch as
Example:
- **Since you are already here,** you may as well study your lessons.

E. **Use of Connectors.** Sometimes there are two or more subjects in a sentence that are connected together by the use of connectors, such as *and, both, not only—but also, or, either—or,* and *neither—nor.*

1. **Use of And.** One of the uses of *and* is to combine two or more subjects in a sentence.
Examples of *and*:

- Michelle **and** Peter went to the store.
- Michelle, Peter, **and** John went to the store.

In the second example, **Michelle, Peter,** and **John** are the subjects and **went** is the verb. Usually, multiple subjects in one sentence are called a *compound subject.*

At the same time, we use *and* to combine two or more subjects of two or more sentences.

Examples:

- Fred wrote a story. Janet wrote a story, too.

  Fred **and** Janet each wrote a story.

- There are pencils on the table. There are books on the table. There are also some crayons and paper on the table.

  There are pencils, books, crayons, **and** paper on the table.

You'll note that a comma is placed between each item in the above example.

Also, we use *and* to combine two or more verbs or actions taken in a sentence.

Examples:

- Secretary Cheney and Brigadier General Powell flew to Saudi Arabia. Later they visited the troops in the desert.

  Secretary Cheney and Brigadier General Powell flew to Saudi Arabia **and** later **visited** the troops in the desert.

Secretary Cheney and **Brigadier General Powell** are the two subjects and **flew** and **visited** are the two verbs or actions in the sentence.

The subject can be the name of a person (or a pronoun)—he or she or whatever), a place (Japan), a thing (doll), or an event (Independence Day).

In a nutshell, two or more subjects, verbs, actions, or thoughts can be combined by *and*.

2. **Use of *Both* and *Not Only...But Also*.** We use *both* in front of two subjects combined, *not only* in front of a sentence, and *but also* at the middle of a sentence.

Examples:

- **Both** Bill and Charley got As in math.
- **Not only** did the bomb destroy the bridge, **but** it **also** damaged the building.

3. **Use of *Or* and *Either...Or*.** The words *or* and *either...or* are used to combine two or more subjects or verbs or actions.

Examples:
- Use a typewriter **or** a computer in writing your report.
- **Either** Peter **or** Michael will go to the high school reunion.

When using the words *or* and *either...or,* make the verb agree
    with the subject closer to the verb.
Examples:
- An air or ground **war** is inevitable.
- Either the father or the **mother** is going to the show.
- Either the father or the **boys** are going to the show.
- The **house** is painted either brown or white.

As you can see in the third example, the word **boys** takes a
plural verb (are) because it is the subject that is closer to the
verb.

4. **Use of *Neither...Nor.*** These two words are used like
either...or. However, they express negative thoughts.

Example:
- **Neither** the boy **nor** the girl is eligible to participate in the
    contest.

Like the use of *either...or,* make the verb agree with the sub-
ject closer to the verb.
Example:
- Neither Johnny nor the **girls** are tall.

As you can see, the word **girls** is closer to the verb *are.*

5. **Combining Two Sentences into One.** Two sentences can
be combined to express related complete thoughts by using
conjunctions *and, but,* and *or.*
Examples:
- Secretary of State Baker flew to the Middle East. He met
    with Arab, Palestinian, and Israeli leaders to solve some
    regional conflicts.
    Secretary of State Baker flew to the Middle East **and** met
    with Arab, Palestinian, and Israeli leaders to solve some
    regional conflicts.
- The negotiations are set for next week. One member of the
    work group will not attend.

The negotiations are set for next week, **but** one member of the work group will not attend.
- Give me death. Or give me money.

Give me death **or** give me money.

F. Semicolons. A semicolon is a punctuation mark that has a period with a comma below it (;). It is used instead of an *and* to join two related complete thoughts or actions. In other words, each thought can stand alone as a sentence.

Example:
- He is too worried now; he is having nightmares.

Sometimes, we use *thus, therefore, however,* and other similar words after a semicolon.
Example:

- He has accomplished all his goals in life; however, he doesn't want to retire from his job yet.

A semicolon is used to precede words such as *for instance, for example,* and *namely,* when they enumerate certain things or actions.
Example:
- Before moving to a new home in a city, you should consider

a number of things; namely, its nearness to a school or a church, its transportation system, and its absence of smog.

G. **Colons.** A colon is used to introduce a list.
Example:
■ The steps are as follows: first, second, third, and so forth.

H. **Appositives.** An appositive is a group of words that identifies or describes a person, a place, a thing, or an event in a sentence. The appositive always follows the word it identifies and is separated by commas from the rest of the sentence.
Examples:

■ Margaret, **a journalist,** wrote the book.
■ Manila, **the Philippines' capital,** was heavily bombarded by Japan during the Second World War.
■ The stealth bomber, **the radar-proof plane**, played a major role in the Dessert Storm War.

II. Sentence Arrangement

In general, the standard English syntax in the structure of a sentence consists of the following:
Subject—verb
subject—verb—modifier
subject—verb—completer (direct object or subject complement)
In other words, in writing a sentence, we usually use the above standard arrangement; for instance, the subject first, then the verb.
Examples:

■ **Arthur talked** slowly.

Arthur is the subject and **talked** is the verb.
■ Arthur **talked slowly.** He cited all the reasons why he didn't go to the party.
■ **Talking slowly,** Arthur cited all the reasons why he didn't go to the party.

As you can see, we used the participial phrase, **Talking slowly,** placed before the subject, **Arthur,** and the other elements of the sentence.

As a good writer, you must vary your sentence structure. You may start a sentence with a subject (Michael, upon learning of his friend's death, flew home to Nevada.) You can also start a sentence with a a conjunction. (Or you may decide to postpone your project.)

In other words, you can also begin sentences with participial, prepositional, or infinitive phrase and other kinds of phrases. The purpose, of course, of pattern change is to write a story or an essay in a continuous flow of thought for clarity and style. Also, changing sentence structure is aimed at avoiding monotonous sentences and/or paragraphs. Also, you must combine short and long sentences. To explain this sentence structure, let's write a biography of a fictitious person and place.

The Story of Saddam Noriega

Saddam Noriega was born and raised in Little Desert, a small town near the city of Bunker, Virgin Islands. His parents were Isidoro Noriega, a farmer, and Milagros de la Riva, a seamstress. They were poor. They lived in a small house made of wood and roofed with dried palm tree leaves.

Saddam sold potatoes from door to door in the nearby city to help his parents cope with the hardships of everyday life. He did this every day, so he was not able to go to school during his entire life. Saddam was taught by his father to read and write in his native tongue. He wanted to be somebody in the future, maybe a leader of his town because he had big dreams.

Etc.

Of course, you can use the above style of writing because some people always write in this manner: subject first, verb second. But that's too monotonous. So you may use different sentence structures. For instance, you may revise the above biography.

The Story of Saddam Noriega

Born and raised in Little Desert, a small town near the City of Bunker, Islands, Saddam Noriega was born to Isidoro Noriega, a farmer, and Milagros de la Rivera, a seamstress. Being poor, they lived in a small house made of wood and roofed with dried palm tree leaves.

To help his parents cope with the hardships of everyday life, Saddam sold potatoes from door to door in the nearby city. Doing this every day, he was not able to go to school during his entire life.

However, Saddam was taught by his father to read and write in his native tongue. For he had big dreams: He wanted to be somebody in the future—maybe a leader of his little town.

As you can see in the revised version, the narration has improved a lot through the interchanging and adding of some words or phrases.

III. Sentence and Paragraph Connections

As a writer, you should know how to write paragraphs and how to connect them like chains so that your essay or story will have a compact flow of thought. (As discussed earlier, a paragraph should contain a single idea or event to be supported by other ideas or events in succeeding paragraphs.)

In an essay, of course, one must first introduce the subject to be discussed. In a short story, you may include in the introductory paragraph the problem that you want to solve in the latter part of your written story.

Then you follow the introductory paragraph with other paragraphs to support your point of view or to narrate the events and actions of characters of your story.

However, paragraphs should have connections. Paragraph two should be connected to paragraph one; three to two, four to three, five to four, and so on—linking them together into a single, cohesive unit to form an essay or a story. This can be done through the use of so-called *transitional devices*.

These transitions fall into three categories:
1. Standard devices
2. Paragraph hooks
3. Combinations of standard devices and paragraph hooks

A. Standard Devices. The following are some examples of standard devices:

At the same time,
Moreover
Consequently
Of course
In general
Admittedly
However
On the other hand
In other words
By and large
Needless to say
But
In addition
Likewise
Even so
Indeed
In fact

Many of the words can be placed at the beginning, middle, and end of sentences and paragraphs.
Examples (in sentences within a paragraph):
■ He didn't say anything. **However**, I could see in his eyes....
■ He is poor. **In fact,** he eats only two times a day.

At the beginning of paragraphs, a writer uses transitional words or phrases, such as *at the same time, on the other hand, in general,* and so forth. Again some words such as *however* and *of course,* may also be located, not only at the beginning of a sentence, but also at middle or end of sentences.

B. **Paragraph Hooks.** Paragraphs can be hooked together by repeating in a paragraph some words used in the last sentence of the preceding paragraph.

Example (used at the end of a paragraph):
■ This can be done with transitional devices.
Example (at the beginning of the next paragraph):
■ Such transitional devices...

Train Cars Are Hooked to Each Other

C. **Combinations of Standard Devices and Paragraph Hooks.** Of course, in an essay or a story, anyone can use transitional words, phrases, or paragraph hooks to connect all the paragraphs.

IV. The Thinking and Writing Processes

The processes used in writing any subject are *sequencing, observing, comparing, classifying, imagining,* and *evaluating.*

A. **Sequencing.** *Sequencing* is the process by which a writer puts ideas and thoughts on paper; for instance, in time and chronological order. In short, the flow of thoughts in an essay or order is in proper sequence, sentence by sentence and paragraph by paragraph. Of course, in a story, a writer sometimes starts with a flashback and then follows the story from beginning to end.

1. *Criteria Sequencing.* Criteria sequencing involves the organization of figures or facts through size, color, height, date, clothing, jobs. etc.

2. *Ranking Sequencing.* Ranking sequencing involves the selection of items or factors according to ranking; for instance, from the biggest to the smallest.

3. *Letter and Word Sequencing.* Letter and word sequencing involves the putting of letters or words in a specific sequence; for example, the proper placement of single words, phrases, and clauses within a sentence.

4. *Event Sequencing.* Event sequencing involves the description of different steps or actions in an essay on events or instructions.

5. *Logical Sequencing.* Logical sequencing involves the teaching of cause-and-effect relationships. Of course, with this process, the effect follows the cause; in other words, for every effect, there's a cause. This process fits well in essays on science and history.

6. *Sentence and Paragraph Sequencing.* Sentence and paragraph sequencing involves putting sentences and paragraphs into proper order; that is, which should be first, second, third, fourth, etc.

B. **Observing.** *Observing* involves the way a writer observes people, animals, places, things, and events for the purpose of describing them on paper.

C. **Comparing.** *Comparing* involves the process by which a writer makes comparison through the use of the so-called figures of speech—similes and metaphors. For example, you may say, "Your lips are like red roses blooming in the midst of spring," or "He is as crazy as Saddam Hussein."

D. **Classifying.** *Classifying* involves sorting items or putting things into certain categories; for instance, similar things (in size, shape, or color) in each category.

E. **Imagining.** *Imagining* requires the writer to create in his reader's mind an image of what he's talking about; for instance, the story's setting, plot, and characterization.

Imagining Creates Visions

F. **Evaluating.** *Evaluating* requires the writer to know how to present facts, opinions, logic, and emotions in order to persuade others to do something or to have belief in his thesis.

1. *Facts and Opinions.* Through this process, the writer should know the difference between facts and opinions.

2. *Persuasive Writing.* For instance, a student may write letters to President Clinton as to why he should not use nuclear weapons to defeat his enemies. Of course, to do so, he should express his valid reasons to prove his point against the use of nuclear weapons.

3. *Emotional Writing Versus Objective Writing.* With this process, the writer evaluates his writing, whether he has appealed to emotions or focused his attention on facts without any emotional appeal.

V. Written Work

A. **Prewriting.** *Prewriting* is the time when you think about what you should write. While thinking about it, you may or may not discuss the matter with your teacher/professor or anybody else. In other words, prewriting is the time when you outline in your mind and on paper what you should be writing.

B. **Drafting.** *Drafting* is when writing actually starts. You may put down on paper what is in your mind; just write, write, and write. The main point is, you should try to put all the important data you want to be included in a descriptive paragraph or story. The commas, periods, and other punctuation marks are just inserted, to be corrected later if there are any mistakes. Grammar, too, should be taken seriously later. When this copy is finished, it's called a rough draft.

C. **Editing**. After you have read your story or short essay, you may reread it or show it to your classmates (or your teacher). Then you may change some words or rearrange some sentences to make the story clearer. That's *editing.*

Writing is an art to be learned, but it can be attained by practice: writing and editing. Practice makes perfect! Who knows? You may become a future Stephen King or Danielle Steele!

Using the Internet to Improve Grades 21

As a student, you can use the Internet to improve your grades. Through it, you can research library catalogs, gain access to encyclopedias, dictionaries, and other references, as well as making friends with other students throughout the world.

In other words, you can surf the Internet and visit web sites, join discussion groups, and communicate with friends, relatives, fellow students, and teachers, anywhere in the world. The beauty of it is, if you have a local service provider that uses local calls, there won't be long-distance phone charges even if you send e-mail (electronic mail) to Bosnia or Russia or somewhere at the North Pole.

In general, the Internet, also known as the information superhighway and cyberspace, is referred to as an electronic medium involving millions of computers communicating with each other through the use of telephone lines and modems. Participants in cyberspace activities are of four kinds of communications networks. They are (1) the Internet, an international communications system in which millions of computer users network with each other worldwide; (2) the commercial online service providers such as CompuServe, America Online, Prodigy, Delphie, and Netcom; (3) the news groups known as Usenet, and (4) the so-called bulletin board services (BBSs).

While the general use of the Internet is the sending and receiving of e-mail, the Internet also refers to the WWW or World Wide Web. Through the WWW, personal, business, and educational web sites are built in cyberspace. These web sites are like catalogs in which services and products are described, displayed, and sold. They are sometimes called cyberspace malls, such as general malls and book malls. They also include information catalogs or sites of government and private institutions, such as the Library of Congress and colleges and universities.

On these web sites, millions of products are sold online through credit card ordering systems. Millions of people also gain access to information that can be gathered from various web sites and through discussion among news groups.

I. Internet Background

The Internet had its beginnings from ARPANET, which was an experimental network in the 1970s that was funded by the U.S. Defense Department to support military research. The military wanted a network that could withstand major outages, such as nuclear attacks. Therefore, ARPANET was designed to be a "distributed" system where the network was considered unreliable (network links can physically or logically go off-line without any warning) and the responsibility for ensuring communications between different network sites was given to "peer-to-peer" computers in the network. The philosophy was that any computer on the network could communicate with any other computer. If a network link between two communicating computers went down then another link, a redundant network path, could be found to re-establish the connection.

II. Internet Protocol

The method of communication (sending a message from one computer and receiving it on another computer) in ARPANET was the Internet Protocol (IP). As the market demand for networking spread and with the success of ARPANET, IP soon became a standard method of communications for network computers. Many manufacturers found that IP was the only suitable protocol for them to use because users individually bought whatever computer they wanted and expected them to work with other computers in a network. This, along with improvements in local area network (LAN) technology, allowed many companies and other organizations to build their own networks.

III. First Internet Highway

In the 1980s, the National Science Foundation (NSF), a U.S. government agency, funded a public network called NFSNET. The purpose for NFSNET was to interconnect supercomputer centers at five major universities. The intent of the NFSNET was to make the resources in the NFS supercomputer centers widely available for use with any scholarly research. Using IP technology from ARPANET, any university in the country could connect to the NFS supercomputer centers. The implementation was as follows: (1) regional networks all across the U.S. were created, (2) schools in a regional network were connected to their nearest neighbor, (3) regional networks were chained together and linked to one of the supercomputer centers, and (4) all the supercomputer centers were connected together with high-capacity and high-speed network links. This configuration allowed any computer to communicate with another computer in the network by using IP technology; for example, messages are forwarded from one computer to the next until the computer to which the IP message was addressed receives it.

NFSNET soon became the first backbone of what is now known as the Internet. As the Internet grew in popularity, both public and private networks—even those that were not based on IP, such as BITNET and DECNET—established network connections to the Internet. These networks wanted to provide the services that were free and publicly available on the Internet to their base users.

IV. Today's Internet

The Internet has become a global network of networks. Physically, the networks are provided for by public and private organizations. Each organization pays for the administration and maintenance of having their network site(s) connected to the Internet. Logically, the networks are linked together into one virtual network. The core of the Internet philosophy is that any computer on a network site can communicate with any other computer.

The Internet works much like the way the global mail system operates. Each country has a public mail network, for example, the United States Postal Service. Mail can be sent internally, within the public network of a country, or externally where mail is forwarded to the public network of the destination country. It is then the responsibility of the public network of the destination country to deliver the external mail within its domain. The mail system also has private networks as well, such as DHL. This is where the network crosses national boundaries and can provide services to its users that may not be available on public networks, e.g., overnight delivery. Users do not need to know how mail is delivered—that is the responsibility of the network providers. They only care about sending mail from one destination to another.

V. Standard Internet Application Services

There are three traditional Internet application standard services: Telnet, File Transfer Protocol, and electronic mail.

A. Telnet is used to establish a communications link between two computers across the Internet. It is generally used to log in from a local computer, such as one that physically located at a company branch office, to a remote computer, that may be physically located 3,000 miles away at the company headquarters. Telnet is a standard protocol that can also be used for customized client/server applications where the local computer is the client and the remote computer is the server. The server computer provides a service, such as a train or bus schedule for a major city, that can be requested from a client computer.

B. Transfer Protocol FTP is a standard protocol used for copying files from one computer to another. It allows any two computers on the Internet to connect and communicate with each other even if they have different native operating systems, for example, DOS and UNIX. FTP uses the same client/server concept as Telnet; for example, a user logs in from the local computer (client) to the remote computer (server) and either downloads files (copies files from the server to the client) or uploads files (copies files from the client to the server).

C. Electronic Mail (E-mail) differs from Telnet and FTP in that it provides "asynchronous service", for instance, communication is not "end to end" where there is a link between two computers and a reply to a message can be immediately received;

rather the user sending the message and not knowing if and when a reply will be received (recall that the network can at times be unreliable and messages can get lost or returned). Depending on the system used, e-mail can be in the form of a simple text message or contain complicated objects in Multipurpose Internet Mail Extensions (MIME) format. As long as both the sender and the receiver are MIME compliant, objects such as image and audio can be sent and received through e-mail.

VI. Internet Business Applications for Selling

The commercial domain is now the fastest growing segment of the Internet. There are thousands of businesses already doing business online—from Fortune 500 companies to sole proprietorships. They sell computer hardware/software, books, airline tickets, and countless other items. The applications used for selling on the Internet include e-mail, Telnet, Gopher, Usenet, and WWW).

A. *E-Mail.* E-mail is a popular method of advertisement for start-up ventures because of its low cost. It is used by companies to provide product information and to accept orders.

B. *Telnet.* Telnet has the look and feel of a bulletin board system (BBS). It can be used to provide an inexpensive customized BBS-type access to the Internet.

C. *Gopher.* Gopher was once the most widely used method of transactions on the Internet. It allows users to browse for information by using menus. FTP is used as an underlying mechanism of Gopher for transferring files containing product information to potential customers. Graphical versions of Gopher exist that a user can use with the "point and click" operations of a mouse.

D. *Usenet.* Usenet, initially created as a platform for discussion groups (more popularly known as newsgroups), has categories for posting advertisements and announcements. In particular, there are for-sale hierarchies used primarily by individuals and small businesses to sell and market merchandise.

E. *World Wide Web*. The WWW is the newest Internet tool. It is very popular because it is easy to interface with the Internet. Browsers, such as Mosaic and Netscape, are used to interactively communicate with the menu system provided by WWW servers. The most popular way for business transactions in WWW is with virtual storefronts/cybermalls.

VII. Internet Methods of Payment

There are three basic methods of payment on the Internet: offline, tokens, and encryption.

Offline is when the consumer makes arrangements by phone, regular mail, or fax. Purchases can then be made by using online input forms or e-mail.

Money can also be exchanged via tokens. Tokens are virtual money bought by consumers to purchase products and services. This form of payment offers flexibility in that consumers do not need to establish an account with each vendor.

Encryption is used to protect sensitive data such as credit card information. Encryption systems have been developed to allow credit card or other data to be sent directly to each vendor through the Internet.

VIII. Connecting to the Internet

The most economical way for small businesses to get connected to the Internet is by subscribing through a service provider. Service providers are like the cable companies. They provide different grades of service, for example, from basic services like e-mail, Telnet, and FTP access to premium services like WWW access and disk quotas. Unlike the cable industry, Internet service providers are in a very competitive market.

The five major online services are as follows:

1.America Online (AOL), 800-827-6364.

2. CompuServe Information Service, 800-848-8199.

3. Delphi, 800-544-4005.

4 Genie, 800-638-9636.

5. Prodigy Interactive Personal Service, 800-776-3449.

Among the five companies, CompuServe Information Service, to some users, is the most international (members from 135 countries) and business-oriented of these services. These companies provide such services as up-to-the minute stock quotes and access to the Internet.

However, there are also many providers that can serve you, although they provide few services. But, like the online services, they can connect you to the Internet and give you the benefits of the Information Superhighway

IX. WWW: Internet Tool

To do business by using the WWW or Web, companies have virtual storefronts where they can build their own sites or lease space on a cybermall. Cybermalls emulate traditional shopping malls by offering a variety of products and services.

To access the WWW, you need a browser program such as Netscape. Netscape can be downloaded from the Internet, free of charge. But you must have a local Internet access provider with a SLIP account. The standard fee is $20.00 for a local service provider. Ask local computer users to recommend a local provider.

When selecting a service provider, keep in mind what features are offered and the costs involved. Consider such factors as the modem connections available, for instance, using a powerful and fast modem. Connecting to the service provider's telephone line locally is less expensive than via a long distance call especially since the call is charged by the minute.

The Internet is the best playing field for small business owners to compete with big companies.

The WWW is the fastest growing technological advance on the Internet. According to some researchers, the Web will eventually become the central marketing center in cyberspace.

Through the Web, you may travel through cyberspace, from country to country or from one web site to another, by pointing and clicking on text, audio, video, or graphics. This is called surfing the Net."

X. Net Surfing

The information superhighway has arrived. Take advantage of its features and services and you can improve your grades.

You may visit educational sites by subjects. Sites may cover all the basics—writing, reading, art, culture, and others.

XI. Educational Sites

You may wish to visit some of these educational sites:

Clip Notes: Offers you access to free things like a *Cliffs Study Tips* disk.

http://www.cliffs.com

Termpapers.on.Line. Gives a different essay monthly. It's free for plagiarizing. You may send an email for a free catalog.

http://www.termpapersonline.com

The WorldWideWeb Virtual Library: Has online literary exhibits.

http://sunsite.unc.edu/ibic/IBIC.homepage.html

The Elementary Grammar: Gives the fundamentals of the English Language.

http://www.hiway.co.uk/~ei/intro.html

The Virtual Writing Laboratory: Is Purdue University's writing lab.

http://owl.english.purdue.edu

A Guide for Writing Research Papers: Is a guide to research and writing.

http://webster.commnet.edu/Library/mla.htm

The Elements of Style: Has the full text of Strunk and White's grammar and composition bible.

http://www.columbia.edu/acis/bartleby/strunk

Online English Grammar: Gives answers for grammatical questions.
http://www.edunet.com/english/grammar/index.html

Math Tips & Tricks: Gives thirty tips and tricks.
http://forum.swarthmore.edu/k12/mathtips/index.html

alt.algebra.help: Is a newsgroup for algebra students.
Usenet alt.algebra.help

A Guide to the Nine Planets: A site about the entire solar system.
http://seds.lpl.arizona.edu

Earth and Universe: Is linked to educational programs about the origin of the universe, stars, the Sun, the galaxy, and others.
http://www.eia.brad.ac.uk/btl
Ins

soc.culture.asian.american: Is a discussion newsgroup.
Usetnet soc.culture.asian.american

Center for the Study of White American Culture. Has links to other resources on white culture.
http://www.euroamerican.org/index.htm

Britannica Online. *Britannica's Year In Review.* Britannica's Encyclopedia online version.
http://www.eb.com

Boston Library Consortium: No library card is required to gain access to the catalogs of Boston College, Boston University, Brandeis, MIT, Northeastern University, Tufts, Wellesleys, UMass/Boston, UMass/Amherst, the Boston Public Library, and the State Library of Massachusetts. Visit this web site for links to these institutions.
Telnet://blc.lrc.northeastern.edu

New York Public Library: Comprises 12 million's volume collection of the world's largest public library.

http://www.nypl.org

To find educational sites, you may do research at sites of so-called search engines.

Some of the leading search engines are located at the following sites:

http://www.altavista.com
http://www.hotbot.com
http://www.excite.com
http://www.yahoo.com
http://www.infoseek.com

Or if you wish to get a comprehensive listings of educational sites, go to your library and see ***Your Personal NetStudy: Your Guide to Getting Better Grades Using the Internet and Online Services*** (Wolff New Media LLC, 520 Madison Avenue, 11th Floor, New York, NY 10022.) If you wish, you may purchase it from your local bookstore.

How to Think Effectively

22

The term "think" covers a wide range of mental operations. According to the dictionary, *think* is the general word meaning to exercise the mental faculties to form ideas and use them for decisions and actions. It may also mean to internally process external responses received by an individual through the senses: *seeing, hearing, smelling, tasting,* and *feeling.*

Needless to say, you should learn how to think, if you want to be able to succeed in school and in life. You need "thinking skills" in subjects such as reading, math, science, and history, especially in the junior high, high school, and college.

In reality, teaching yourself to develop thinking skills is a complex procedure. In fact, thinking experts and school teachers use different approaches to teaching students how to think. There are major thinking skills and subskills, and some of them overlap each other.

I. Basic Thought Groups

Most authors agree that in thinking, five basic thought groups are used: *input, retrieval, processing, output,* and *decision and action.*

A. **Input:** *Gathering Data.* The gathering of information to be stored in the brain involves the senses: *seeing, hearing, smelling, tasting,* and *feeling,* which, of course, are accomplished by the eyes, ears, nose, tongue, and skin.

Use this process, ask some questions such as:

Seeing: "What is the man doing?"
Hearing: "What is your friend saying?"
Smelling: "How does the fruit smell?"
Tasting: "How does the mango taste?"
Feeling: "Are you cold?"

B. **Retrieval:** *Recalling information.* You may provide state-ments to yourself to help you draw ideas, inferences, or conclu-sions from the facts, feelings, responses, or experiences acquired in the past and imbedded in the short- or long-term memory.

To retrieve facts or information from your short- or long-term memory, you should be able to participate in some activities, such as *naming, describing, identifying, listing,* and *recalling.*
Examples:

Naming: "What are the New England states?"
Describing: "Describe what happened in the meeting."
Listing: "List the things you'll bring to class."

C. **Processing:** *Organizing or grouping of facts and informa-tion gathered from short- or long-term memory.* The evaluation should be based on processes such as *summarizing, sequenc-ing, finding cause-and-effect, relationships, categorizing, sorting, analogy making, classifying,* and *synthesizing.*
Examples:

Summarizing: "Can you summarize the first chapter of the book?"
Classifying: "What are the seven classification groups of plants and animals?"
Sequencing: "Please arrange the numbers in sequence."

Again, the senses play major parts in drawing the above pro-cesses from the information stored in your biocomputer. To attain them, you must make some statements or ask some questions that may lead to the above processes.

D. **Output:** *Evaluating facts.* Explain or give reasons for the cause of any results of an observation or an experimentation based on available information.

To help obtain results from evaluation, you should apply some of the following processes: *evaluating, generalizing, spec-ulating, contrasting,* and *investigating.*

Examples:

Speculating: "Can you speculate what the hero will do in the next chapter?"

Evaluating: "Evaluate the solution to the problem based on the given facts."

Generalizing: "What are the characteristics of amphibians?"

E. **Decision and Action:** *Making decisions and taking actions.* You can make a decision and take action based your evaluation of given facts.

Examples of skills needed in conclusion are *inferring* and *interpreting.*

Inferring: "What evidence can you cite that proves that he has made the wrong decision?"

Interpreting: "Give your own opinion on what he said."

A conclusion may be made based on different situations. For instance, when you have already evaluated the problem or the current situation, you have to conclude what the situation is or what action should be taken. Then you must decide and act!

For example, when you are trying to solve a math problem, you must take the following steps:

1. Do the data gathering (the known facts and what the problem is or what is to be solved).

2. Name or identify the facts and know the formula to be used or steps to be taken to know the "unknown."

3. Sequence the steps to be taken based on past experiences in solving math problems.

4. Make the judgment whether they are really the steps to be taken and then act to solve the problem.

These thinking processes may also be used in other subjects, such as reading comprehension, science experiments, and historical analysis. However, they may be done in different procedures.

II. Complex Categories of Thinking

Authors mention different categories of thinking. Some of the most known and important kinds of thinking are *critical think-*

ing, creative thinking, deductive thinking, and *inductive think-ing.*

It's hard to define the functions of "thinking" processes because sometimes they overlap each other. But we'll try to define each of them simply and concisely.

A. **Critical Thinking.** Critical thinking may be defined as the critical analysis and evaluation of beliefs on an issue or issues and the actions to be taken. Sometimes it may involve various reasons on both sides of a case or an issue. Sometimes, it may involve the use of imagination to analyze the facts or details of a given situation. Of course, it may also involve speculation of causes or courses of action.

Some of the usual critical thinking skills are as follows:

1. *Recognition and Recalling.* These are the processes of naming, matching, sorting, ordering, connecting, or relating things or events. For instance, you may teach yourself to name things: name the things inside the house; match the two sets of balls; put the numbers in order, etc.

2. *Distinguishing and Visualizing.* These are the processes by which you may solve problems in more systematic and correct ways. That is, you must distinguish the things or the events in certain situations, and you must learn how to visualize the correct procedures to help solve the problem.

3. *Classifying.* This is the process by which objects, living things, and nonliving things are grouped together into certain classes, according to their similarities and differences in sizes, shapes, and colors.

4. *Sequencing and Predicting.* These are the processes by which objects, things, and events are arranged in sequence. They also involve the predicting of what may happen based on the results of observation and inferences.

5. *Analyzing.* This is the process by which you break up a whole into its small parts or steps to find the solution of a problem or learn its important features. For instance, you may determine the main ideas and the sub-ideas. By analyzing the parts of a theory, a story or a math problem, you may understand the whole when you break it into small parts or steps to find the solution of a problem.

6. *Evaluating:* It is the process of forming an opinion on certain cases, issues, or situations to know whether the steps to be taken are the right ones.

7. *Inferring and Drawing Conclusions:* These are the processes by which you explain your observations of certain things or events and make your conclusions about them based on what you have observed, studied, and learned.

B. **Creative Thinking.** Creative thinking involves the creation of a complex product such as a story, a machine, or a theory. One of the skills involved in creative thinking is *synthesizing,* which is the processes by which you may combine ideas from available sources or in different ways to create new ideas or products. You may develop a new product based on existing products.

The functions of critical thinking and creative thinking overlap each other. Critical thinking results in ideas through creative thinking, while there are also times when creative thinking needs ideas from critical thinking to create a product.

Critical thinking and creative thinking are different in the sense that while critical thinking involves a critical assessment of a belief or an action, creative thinking involves the creation of a product. Both of these skills, however, require new facts or details to be analyzed and used.

C. **Deductive Thinking.** Deductive thinking involves the presenting of the generalization to a group; for example, to support data, cases, or evidence. It also involves seeking additional data.

D. **Inductive Thinking.** Inductive thinking involves the collection, organization, examination of data and the identification of common or general elements. The purpose, of course, is to check the data to see if the "generalization" stands.

In general, deductive (from the general to the specific) and inductive (from the specific to the general) are the two types of inference in drawing conclusions.

Develop these skills and subskills in you, and you'll know how to accumulate knowledge and how to use it to be a success in school.

7-Point Formula to Be an Honor Student   23

A formula is a method or system for making or doing things; it is the key to an objective. Used efficiently, a formula for success will help you achieve your major goal of becoming an honor student.

I've devised a seven-point formula based on my experience and on examples from case studies of other successful students. You may adopt this success formula to help you succeed to become an honor student.

I. Have a Dream and Chase It

A woman friend of mine once asked me what she should first do to launch her dream to become an a successful business-woman. My answer was, "Have a dream and chase it!"

Yes, a dream results from ambition, and without ambition, there is nothing to look forward to and aim for in the future.

What is ambition? Webster's New World Dictionary defines ambition as "a strong desire to gain a particular objective; specif., the drive to succeed, or to gain fame, power, wealth, etc."

To have a dream, you must ignite your booster rockets for ambition!

Do you want to become an honor student and later to become an author? A graphic designer? A consultant? An importer-exporter? A seminar speaker? A global entrepreneur? What is stopping you from launching a dream to succeed? Are you deaf? Beethhoven, composer of immortal symphonies, was deaf. Are you crippled? Alexander Pope was crippled so pain-fully that he could hardly move, but he became a Goliath of English literature! The list goes on and on!

II. Program Your Mind for Success

You should program your mind for success. All mankind's achievements originate in the mind.

Program your mind for success so you can develop a positive mental attitude, ignite your booster rocket for ambition, and have high self-esteem, faith in yourself, enthusiasm, and persistence—all of which are the nuts and bolts for achieving success.

III. Set Short-Term Goals and Long-Term Goals and Make Plans to Accomplish Them

If you already have a burning desire to become a successful student, you must make plans and work according to those plans. An architect makes a plan for a house or a building. You, too, should make plans to improve your grades and become a smart student.

A. *Mastering Your Fate.* Whether you're in your teens or twenties, remember what poet William Ernest Henley wrote: "I am the master of my fate, I am the captain of my soul."

So don't let yourself float like a log, swept here and there in the river of no return. Paddle your own canoe!

When you prepare your short- and long-term goals, be specific about what you want to be; whether you want to be a part-time or full-time student.

When you prepare your short- and long-term goals, be specific about what you want to become, whether you want to be a lawyer or a doctor or whatever.

B. *Planning.* Now you must make plans. Prepare a studying plan. Specifically, the plan should include the following steps:

1. A description of how you should launch your dream of becoming an honor student.

2. An evaluation of your present situation. Are you getting Cs and Ds, instead of As and Bs in class? What resources do you have? What skills do you have? How would you reinforce your past experiences and knowledge?

3. A step-by-step procedure on how you should implement your plan.

4. A deadline for accomplishing your goals.

C. *Start Now!* Whatever resources you have, whatever interests and abilities you have or you don't have, you must start now! Survey the competition—how your classmates or friends are doing. Develop a plan of accomplishments that you'll enjoy.

Remember, in launching a dream of becoming an honor student, you're like a hunter who goes to an unchartered territory to hunt for deer (or whatever). Arm yourself with the proper hunting tools and equipment. As a student, you'll master the basics of subjects and techniques of studying and test taking.

IV. Make Use of Smart Technology

With today's advanced technology (computer, fax machine, voice mail, etc.), you can become an honor student. Use today's advanced technology, including the Internet, for your research and other resources for studying.

V. Form Alliances with Other Students

As a student, you may wish to form an alliance with classmates (two or three, four, or five) in pursuing studying goals. For instance, if you're good at science but not so good at math, you may form a partnership in studying with a friend who's good at math. Then as a good student at science, you may have a bargaining tool with friends or students not doing good in this subject.

In other words, you may form alliances with other students, forming a small group devoted to enhancing your knowledge and expertise in different subjects.

VI. Use the Brains and Experiences of Other People

As a wise student, receive free and paid advice from students or other people. You may be able to receive constructive criticism or feedback from a mentor if you can find one.

VII. Simplify Your Studying Methods

One of the reasons why some students are afraid to launch a dream of becoming an honor student is that they have no belief in their ability. Some of them are reluctant to master the basics of major subjects. First, learn the fundamentals of studying and learning, and you'll have confidence in your ability. Pursue your dream with determination and perseverance.

Simplification is the best tool for a smart student who wants to become an honor student. For instance, simplify your systems in note taking, memorizing, and summarizing. As noted in one of the chapters, tape your important notes and memorize them while driving a car or before going to asleep. Listen to the tapes, instead of counting sheep when you can't fall asleep.

Brief Summary, More Strategies   24

In this chapter. we present a summary of some tips and strategies mentioned in this book. And, of course, we've added some more studying techniques and overall strategies to become an honor student.

I. Keys to Memorization

■ You must be able to use images and word codes that serve as the keys to quick retention and recall. Concrete objects can easily be transformed into pictures.

■ In memorization, you may use certain systems, such as letter codes, rhyming, and sound-alike words.

■ When you're memorizing information, take a word or two from each sentence or paragraph and form another sentence or story to link the main and secondary ideas.

II. Note Taking

■ Sit in front of the room. If other people beat you to the front row, try to take a seat in the second, third, fourth, or fifth row (if you're not seated in alphabetical order). If you do this, you are more likely to hear what the teacher/instructor presents.

■ Listen through your eyes, your ears, and your mind.

■ Take notes when you listen. Watch your teacher's body language, and you'll know what part of the lecture is important.

■ Listen to the teacher's vocabulary, and you'll know what should be and what should not be written down. Take note of these phrases: *The main causes of...the most important events during the war,* etc.

■ Organize your notes with a clear structure. Taking notes is not just making a list.

■ Create your own symbols and abbreviations.

■ Underline only a few important words.

■ Organize your information into groups or classifications; that is, similar subjects in a group.

■ Don't miss a class because you'll miss those important lectures. If it does happen, don't forget to copy notes taken by a friend or classmate.

III. Test Taking

■ Budget your time. Allocate certain seconds or minutes to a question. For example, if the test is required to be done in one hour, divide it by the number of questions and you'll arrive at the number of seconds or minutes to be allocated to a question.

■ Answer the easiest questions first.

■ Ask the teacher questions if you are not sure about the directions.

■ Guess when you don't know the answer, except when the test stipulates any punishment such as right minus wrong answers.

■ Change your answers with care. Most of the time, your first hunch is the correct answer.

■ Guess when you don't know the answers on standardized tests, for example, "all of the above."

■ Be careful when you see the words, *usually, sometimes, often, most of the time, always* and similar words. Such words usually conveys that you're being "tricked."

IV. Efficient Reading

■ *Previewing.* In previewing a book, you read the title, the subtitle, and the author's name, the table of contents, the bold-faced headings, the italicized words, the subheadings, the introduction, the afterword, the appendix, the index, and some of the maps, graphs, charts, and illustrations. Previewing is especially useful for getting a general idea of nonfiction books, or magazine or newspaper articles.

■ *Skimming.* Skimming is reading quickly and lightly, searching for factual information.

- *Scanning.* Scanning is a quick, orderly lookout for key words or phrases.
- *Digesting.* Digesting is the slowest type of reading; you must grasp ideas and thoughts.

V. Effective Studying

In 1946, Dr. Francis P. Robinson devised a study system known as SQ3R. The system is as follows:

- *Survey.* Read the chapter heading and subheads, the introductory and summary paragraphs, and the review questions.
- *Question.* Ask questions about the chapter heading and subjects, seeking answers to *how* and *why*, etc.
- *Read.* Grasp ideas and thoughts from the printed page of your handwritten notes to find answers to your questions.
- *Recite.* Close your book or notes. Then close your eyes or look out the window and recite the items, answering questions.
- *Review* Close your book or notes again, and answer the questions you've asked yourself, giving a general review of the whole assignment or books and notes in preparation for a test.

VI. Seven-Point Formula for Becoming an Honor Student

The following seven points, when practiced, will help you to become an honor student.

1. *Have a dream and chase It.* To have a dream, you must ignite your booster rockets for ambition!

2. *Program your mind for success.* You can develop a positive mental attitude, and have high self-esteem, faith in hourself, enthusiasm, and persistence.

3. *Set short-term and long-term goals and make plans to accomplish them.* If you already have a burning desire to become a successful student, you must make plans and work according to those plans.

4. *Make use of smart technology.* With today's advanced technology (computer, fax machine, etc.), you can become an honor

student.

5. *Form alliances with other students.* As a student, you may form an alliance with a friend or friends (one or several) in pursuing studying goals.

6. *Use the brains and experiences of other people.* As a wise student, receive free and paid advice from other students or people. You may be able to receive constructive criticism or feedback from a mentor if you can find one.

7. *Simplify your studying methods.* Learn the fundamentals of studying and learning as outlined in this book.

Part IV

**Be the Best
You Can Be**

Positive Attitude: The Key to Success 25

Thoughts occupy your mind: they are powerful enough to uplift your spirit and emotions or to paralyze you into immobility. If you're in control of your thoughts, you'll be in control of your emotions, dreams, and destiny. Either you think positively or you think negatively; it's as simple as that. If you're a positive thinker, you'll move forward, however big the obstacles are. If you're a negative thinker, you're doomed to fail.

You can think positively if you dwell on past successes and not on failures; if you see the bright side of life and not the dark side; if you look at problems as opportunities, think only about things that you can change, and forget about things you can't change. You can change the way you think, from negative to positive; you can improve your grades. You can exercise your mind just as you exercise your muscles.

Thoughts Occupy Your Mind

Expand your vocabulary to include phrases such as: *I can do it; it's hard but I can make it; nothing under the sun is impossible; if they did it, I can do it, too.* If you can do that, you'll be a positive thinker.

Wherever you were born, wherever you were raised, and whatever your family background is, you can excel in class and be whatever you want to be if you think you can. The secret is a positive attitude.

The 'I Can Do It' Attitude

One day, nine-year-old Brenda Turney sat in her wheelchair facing a video screen and reading a magnified version of her textbook in her elementary school class in Battle Creek, Michigan. Brenda, who had cerebral palsy and had difficulty in reading small print, stopped suddenly at a certain word. "We're not allowed to say that word," she told her teacher's assistant. The word was *can't.*

In the Ann J. Kellogg Elementary School, students have been told that there is nothing they cannot do. The *I can do it* attitude adopted by the school has made it one of Michigan's 13 outstanding elementary schools and one of 270 in the nation. (These schools were recognized at a ceremony held at the White House.) The results show that the plan works. The Kellog School set reading skills and an increase in parent involvement as the priorities for improving the school's standard of education. From the 1983-84 to the 1984-85 school year, the percentage of fourth graders who passed the state's reading assessment test rose from 36 to 66 percent.

'No Speak' English

Several years ago, Maou Yang lost his home when his family fled from the Communists in Laos. He lost not only his home and country but also his voice; he could not speak a word of English when he arrived here as a refugee.

"Not knowing the language, it's just like you're a little child and people can't hear you," said Yang, now 18. "Once I learned the language I started becoming a person again. Then people said, 'He's not so dumb.'"

For five years, with persistence and determination, Yang learned English as his second language. Yang's first language is Hmong, one of the native tongues of Laos.

"No matter how tough it is, I never give up if it's right and true to me," he said. "You just can't say, 'I can't do that.'"

Yang always said, *"I can,"* and he could! In 1987 he graduated from the Sexton High School in Lansing, Michigan with a 3.2 grade-point average and won a scholarship to Michigan Technological University.

One thing is sure: if Yang hadn't learned English and if he hadn't excelled in class, he could not have won a scholarship and attended a college of his choice. His dreams would have been in vain. If he did it, you can do it, too.

The Flunker Turned Smarter

W. Clement Stone tells this story in his book, *The Success System That Never Fails* (reprinted by permission of the publisher, Prentice-Hall, Englewood Cliffs, NY):

> This story reminds me of the case history of a boy I know who almost flunked in every grade in grammar school. As a teenager, he was lucky enough to be passed through high school. As a freshman at the state university, he flunked out the first semester.
>
> He was a failure—but that was good, for it developed inspirational dissatisfaction within him. He knew he had the ability to succeed, and on reflection he realized that he had to change his attitude and work hard to make up for lost time.
>
> With this new right mental attitude, he entered a junior college, and he did work hard. He kept trying. And on graduation day, he received the honor of being second highest in class.
>
> No, he didn't stop there. He applied for admission to one of the nation's leading universities, where scholastic standards are exceedingly high and admission is the most difficult to obtain. When the Dean of Men wrote in his response to his application for admission to the university, he asked, "What happened? How do you account for your success at a junior college after failure for so many years?" The boy responded:
>
> "At first, it was real work for me to study regularly, but after several weeks of daily effort, study time became a habit. It became natural for me to study at regular periods. And there were times when I actually looked forward to it, for it was fun to be a 'somebody' at school and be recognized for my scholastic record.
>
> "I aimed to be the best in class. Perhaps it was the shock of being flunked out in my freshman year at the University of

Illinois that awakened me. That's when I began to grow up. I just had to prove to myself that I had the ability."

Because of his right mental attitude and his record of achievement at junior college, this young man was admitted to the university—and there, too, he developed an enviable record.

Old People Learn New Tricks

Too old to study? Too old to pursue your dreams?

Francisco Padolina, who was in a private law practice in the Philippines for 18 years, arrived here as an immigrant in 1979. At the age of 58, he was told that he had to go back to school to become eligible to take the bar exam so he could practice law in the United States.

Instead, Padolina decided to pursue an education in another field. His relatives — even his immediate family — told him that he was too old to study. Many people discouraged him, but he persisted. In 1983 he received an associate degree in mental health from Camden County College in Blackwood, New Jersey, and in 1986 he earned a bachelor of science in social work from Rutgers University in Camden. To top it off, he ranked number five in a Social Worker 2 examination given by the State of New Jersey in 1987. Thus, at the age of 65, he was promoted to Social Worker 2 at a hospital in New Jersey.

How did he do it? When interviewed, Padolina said that to excel in class and on examinations, he used study techniques and test-taking strategies similar to those described in this book. He attributes his success particularly to "outlining" and to searching for the main and secondary ideas in every paragraph of every chapter or section of an article or a book. If he did it, you can do it, too!

When I went back to college at the age of 33, my classmates were at ages 18 through 25 years old. They were young and energetic, and they had all day to study. I was the oldest in class, so it would have been a shame if I hadn't done well. My time was divided: I had to work almost the whole day, and I had to go to class in the evening. I had to spend a short time with my family at night before I studied my lessons. Time was limited, so I was forced to think of the fastest ways to memorize and the easiest ways to learn. From certain books I got some ideas on how to study. I also devised some study methods of my own, including strategies for memorization and reading. I developed self-confidence, and I recited well in front of my classmates. As a result I was included on the honor roll, for the first time in my life!

There's nothing you can't do if you want to do it. Just change your attitude from negative to positive. As soon as negative thoughts enter your mind, replace them with positive thoughts. Then you'll believe in yourself and you'll awaken the sleeping genius within you. From now on, if you're not doing it yet, take steps to become a good student. If you have high grades, you're on your way to your dreams: the college of your choice and the career that you want. If you're already in college, continue reading this book and you'll see how easy it is to scrutinize, assimilate, and digest thoughts for easy learning. With patience and commitment, you'll develop a master plan for your fate!

26

Raising Your Self-Esteem: The Key to Self-Fulfillment

Self-esteem may be defined simply as "You are what you think you are." All of us have self-esteem, but the degree depends on how we regard our own feelings: how we blame and hate ourselves when we make mistakes, and how we love and reward ourselves when we are successful.

You may have low, average, or high self-esteem. Since self-esteem is a conglomeration of all your feelings towards yourself, other people and life itself, you must develop high self-esteem to have the self-respect and self-confidence so necessary in becoming a successful student and a successful human being. In view of this, you should shield yourself from negative feedback: from your friends and enemies, your parents and teachers, and all the people you encounter throughout the day, every day.

They may say to you, "You aren't smart," "You're worth nothing," "You always make mistakes," "You can't do it," or "You'll never learn." When you hear these words, try to put an invisible plug in your ears; don't let those words penetrate your subconscious mind. If you do, you're letting other people control your life; you're a victim of other people's emotions and frustrations.

The lower your self-esteem, the more you'll have negative thoughts and think of failures; the more you'll feel down and believe you have nothing to live for; the more you'll think that you can't be a success in life.

On the other hand, the higher your self-esteem, the more ambitious and enthusiastic you'll be to set goals to pursue your dreams; the more you'll feel that you're entitled, like any anybody else, to success and happiness.

In the early 1970's, a father would throw his son a baseball. The son would catch it, and throw the ball back to his father. That became a daily routine. There was nothing unusual about it, except that the son had no right hand! He would catch the ball, flip his glove into his handless forearm, and throw the ball back to his father.

An ordinary human being would not dare to do what this young man envisioned in life, but he had high-self-esteem; he believed in his ability and potential and his parents believed in him. He was not ashamed of himself just because of his handicap; he believed that he could accomplish whatever he dreamed of doing.

As a pitcher, Jim Abbott led the University of Michigan baseball team to two Big Ten championships. He also pitched for the United States in the Pan American Games, humiliating Cuba in Havana, and pitched for the U.S. team in the Seoul Olympics, where the Americans became world champions.

The left-handed Abbott was drafted by the California Angels. One day in March 1989, at age 21, he stood on the mound in the Oakland A's spring training park in Phoenix; he had two strikes on batter Jose Canseco, one armed pitcher against slugger. Abbott threw the next pitch and Canseco swung and missed! On that day, Abbott became a winning pitcher for the first time as a professional. He dreamed it, and he made it! He is a positive thinker with high self-esteem!

Many people are not like Jim Abbott, however. Because they were born with a disability, because they were born not intelligent, or because they were born poor, they let others abuse them physically and mentally. Their lack of self-confidence erodes their thinking and interferes with their ability to set goals for themselves. Many people can't handle the failures in school or in personal relationships that diminish their self-worth and self-respect. It's too hard for them to learn from their mistakes and to go on living! For this reason, such people succumb to drugs and deep depression which sometimes drive them to end their lives.

People with high self-esteem think that failures are only temporary defeats. They feel that they can bounce back from their failures and disappointments.

Self-Acceptance

Look at yourself in the mirror. Maybe you like most of what you see, but maybe you don't like everything. Try to love what you have; accept yourself as you are! There is only one you in this world. You're unique! You're the only one in the world who has exactly your physical features and exactly your intricately wired brain.

Dr. Lilia S. Mangulabnan, a psychiatrist who practices in Birmingham, Michigan, has given the following tips for raising your self-esteem:

- Make an inventory of your assets and liabilities and strengths and weaknesses.
- Break free from negative self-concept and self-destructive behavior to free yourself from guilt.
- Take responsibility for your own goals to achieve success, and stop blaming other people or outside circumstances for your failures.
- Be able to accept yourself with all the positive and negative aspects of your life.
- Find the courage to love yourself and to nurture the self-esteem of other people.

Love Yourself and Your Neighbor

Onward to Your Destiny!

Time and time again, psychiatrists and psychologists have advised us that if other people are to respect us, we have to respect ourselves first. Treat yourself well and other people will treat you well.

Be responsible for your thoughts and actions. If you make mistakes, forgive yourself, admitting that you're only human and that you'll learn from those mistakes.If you do the right things, then you can reward yourself.

As you achieve successes based on what you've planned— earning high grades, winning a school contest, or making the baseball team—you'll feel that you're raising your self-esteem. As your self-esteem grows you'll know that you're becoming happier and friendlier and more content with life—an individual who has a mission to accomplish.

As you accomplish what is best for you, dreaming the right dreams, setting the right goals for yourself, and making the right choices, you'll know that there's a purpose in your life, and your self-esteem will raise further. You'll let go the guilty feelings about your mistakes, and you'll experience the fullness, not the emptiness, of life. No more blaming others, no more procrastination, no more backward thinking. What is left is peace of mind and your plan for your future. Like others, you're qualified for a place in society and entitled to success and happiness, but it all depends on your own way of thinking. You're what you think you are, and you'll become whatever you want to become! Onward to your destiny!

Setting Short-Term and Long-Term Goals 27

If you already have a burning desire to become whatever you want to be, you must make plans and work according to those plans. A surveyor plans his work and works his plan with an instrument; an architect makes a plan for a house or building, complete with sketches, facts, and figures: a description of each room, details of the materials to be used, costs of labor and materials, the number of workers needed to complete the edifice. You, too, should make plans.

Plan Your Work and Work Your Plan

Where Are You Going?

During my first days in America, I asked a woman who was walking on the street, "Where are you going?" She looked at me, puzzled. I asked a man the same question and he answered, "It's none of your business!" In my native town of General Tinio, Nueva Ecija, in the Philippines, when you meet a man or a woman on the road or anywhere else, you don't greet him or her with "How are you?" You ask, "Where are you going?" or "Where have you been?"

Now I ask you, where are you going? What do you want to become? Why not set short-term and long-term goals? Short-term goals may be goals for a day, a month, or a year. Long-term goals may be goals for two years, five years, or ten years. Think small and you'll get small things; think big and you'll get big things. Read the following lines, and you'll know what I mean:

Where Are You Going?

I bargained with Life for a penny,
    And Life would pay no more,
However I begged at evening
    When I counted my scanty store.

For Life is just an employer,
    He gives you what you ask,
But once you have set the wages,
    Why, you must bear the task.

I worked for a menial's hire,
    Only to learn, dismayed,
That any wage I had asked of Life,
    Life would have willingly paid.

—Anonymous

Write Down Your Goals

Write down your short-term and long-term goals. For instance, if you're now in the first year of high school, you can set your goals; if you're an average student, plan how you can improve your grade-point average for each year. When you graduate you can have high grades, high enough to qualify you to enter the college or university of your choice and to pursue the career and travel the route you designed in your mind.

The Clock Is Ticking

Your short- and long-term goals should include the time at which you'll accomplish what you want, the career you want to pursue, and the exact amount of money you want to accumulate by the time you reach the age of 55 or whatever age you choose. Don't forget to set a deadline for your goals.

Make a general written statement of destiny to read before you go to sleep and when you wake up. The idea of writing a statement was conceived first by Napoleon Hill in *Think and Grow Rich*, one of the most influential books ever published. Other writers of self-help books have adopted this idea, although they presented it in different ways.

Write Down Your Goals

When you have written your statement, don't show it to your classmates, to your wife or husband (if you're married), or to your boss (if you're employed). If you do, they may think you're crazy, so this is just between you and me. Read it aloud twice daily; feed it to your subconscious mind. Believe and feel as if you already possess the money. Later you won't need to read the statement; you'll be able to recite it because you'll have memorized it. When you read or recite such a statement it penetrates into the depths of your body and brain, giving it to the subconscious mind to work on even while you're asleep.

Your statement may be something like the one I prepared years ago when I was publishing books in my native land. My statement reads:

> I, Veltisezar B. Bautista, do hereby declare that I'll be a millionaire at the age of 60, accumulating the sum of at least five million. There is no something for nothing. I'll get this money by giving service to humanity, publishing books to help people improve their lives. So help me God.

This statement gives me a definite purpose in life and increases my courage and determination in whatever I do. I recite it like a prayer before and after sleeping. Then I pray to God for strength of body and mind to accomplish this dream. I always play my success on the screen of my imagination: I see happy buyers reading my books; I see my distributors selling my books to thousands of customers; every day I receive checks in the mail. I see the checks with my own eyes, I touch them, I smell them, and I see myself or my wife going to the bank. I don't know if this is craziness or what. Many people, particularly Napoleon Hill, say that this system works. I think it does.

Did I accomplish my dream of being a millionaire? In 1990, I made my first $100,000 annual sales in book publishing. If I had gone to the Philippines and converted the U.S. dollars into Philippine pesos, I would have been a millionaire. Mission accomplished!

Yes, I became a millionaire in pesos while still in my fifties. I must confess, though, that I made a mistake. I just emphasized to my mind (in my every night statement of faith while still in the Philippines), that I would become a millionaire. I didn't, however, clarify the millions should be in dollars and not in pesos.

You're the Master of Your Fate

Whether you're in your teens, your twenties, or your fifties, remember what poet William Ernest Henley wrote: "I am the master of my fate, I am the captain of my soul." Don't let yourself float like a log, swept here and there in the River of No Return. Paddle your own canoe! Some time ago my father-in-law, 73, wrote me and said that he was lonely and miserable. I advised him to make his own destiny, and he did! He got married for the third time.

Don't Let Yourself Float like a Log....

You can start to set goals even at an early age. A 10-year-old boy from Detroit has set his goals and knows where he's going. "I think I'm going to go a long way in art," he says. "I don't know why but I think I will. I think I shouldn't waste my talent. I want to be a real famous painter someday. My teachers tell me I am a good artist but I get shy about it."

This boy, Clarence Stallworth, a positive thinker and a goal setter, was one of 58 Michigan students honored as winners of the essay and art contest sponsored by the State Board of Education's Bicentennial of the U.S. Constitution. He won first prize for the kindergarten through third grade level in the mixed media art category with a drawing of fireworks.

Clarence has taken the first steps, and he's on the way to making his own destiny!

When you prepare your short- and long-term goals, be specific about what you want: whether you want to have a career and be employed for the rest of your life, or to be employed in the early years of your life and be on your own in middle or later life. You might also want to be self-employed and go into business after you graduate from college.

The following lines may give you some inspiration and motivate you to prepare your goals. (A copy of this is hanging on a wall in my bedroom.)

An American Creed

I do not choose to be a common man. It is my right to be uncommon if I can. I seek opportunity—not security. I do not wish to be a kept citizen: humbled, dulled, by having the State look after me. I want to take the calculated risk; to dream and build; to fail or succeed. I refuse to barter incentive for a dole.

I prefer the challenge of life to the guaranteed existence; the thrill of fulfillment to the state calm of utopia.

I will not trade freedom for benevolence, nor my dignity for a handout. I will never cower before any master nor bend to any threat. It is my heritage to stand erect, proud, and unafraid; to think and act for myself; enjoy the benefits of my creation, and to face the world boldly and say:

This, I have done!

—Anonymous

Now it's time to prepare your written short-term and long-term goals in life. You'll have a definite route to follow and you'll reach your destiny! I'll see you there.

Ignite Your Booster Rocket for Ambition 28

Almost a century ago, people recognized that rocket power was the key to the exploration of space beyond the earth's atmosphere. Vehicles cannot be sent into space against the force of gravity without the use of powerful rockets.

To be a success in life, to do what you want to do, you need booster rockets to send your dreams into your own outer space. You need a burning desire. Do you want to be a doctor? an engineer? a scientist? a computer programmer? Do you want cars, a yacht, a big house, and a lot of money to enjoy the rest of your life?

You can be whatever you want to be, but first things first. You need to have a good education and to acquire knowledge to survive in this dog-eat-dog world. That's why you have to make high grades so that you'll be admitted to a good college or university; if you don't, the only place you can go is to a low-standard college. It's a fact; if you're a graduate of Harvard, Standard, or Yale, you don't need to look for a job. The jobs look for you.

"How can I ignite my booster rocket from within me?" you may ask. It's easy. Think big and be ambitious! Think of the career you'll build, the money you'll accumulate, or the fame you'll achieve, and the booster rockets in your brain will launch your dreams. Then chase those dreams!

The Dreamers

Why did my family and I come to America? Because my wife wanted to further her study and training to be a successful physician; I wanted to seek fame and fortune as a writer; and we wanted our children to have a better education and a better life.

We came here in 1976 and rented an old apartment in the southwestern part of Detroit. The apartment was okay for us, but during spring and fall, when it rained, it poured. When we arrived, we had no relatives to lean on, no money, no jobs waiting for us, no TV, no Pac-Man. We didn't have those things, but we had one important ingredient of success: a *dream*. The dream was launched from our minds and it lives on; after struggling to study for several though examinations, which she took 20 years after graduating from college, my wife is now a successful physician.

When I told some of my friends that I wanted to write and publish books in America, they laughed at me. A woman who's involved in selling books warned me that I would lose my shirt because I was too small to compete with the giant publishers in America. I didn't hear them: my desire was as hot as a glowing iron. No one could stop me. I failed during my first years of writing and self-publishing; few people bought my instant-printed and home-produced booklets on postal exams. Bookstores would not buy it; my friends and relatives would not buy it (they wanted to get it free). But I persisted, for I had faith in myself and in my product.

After five years, when I had enough money, I bought a computer, rewrote the manuscript, and produced it in book form. Then I had the opportunity to contact the big book distributors that now sell my book to bookstores and libraries. My first book, *The Book of U.S. Postal Exams*, has gone to press many times. My distributors have sold thousands of copies beyond my wildest dreams. It was then I realized that in order to succeed in life, you need the help of other people. You can't do it alone. You must share the job and you must share the rewards!

Now I'm writing and publishing self-help books so I can help others succeed in life. The American dream lives on: my children, who have a good educational foundation and a burning desire, have excelled in the classroom, using effective study and test-taking techniques. (One of them finished high school in three years and finished his four-year B. S. Chemistry course in two years, graduating *summa cum laude* from the University of Michigan.) The important thing that we all have is *desire* — a burning desire to succeed.

Are You Deaf? Crippled? It Doesn't Matter!

What is stopping you from launching a dream to succeed? Are you deaf? Beethoven, composer of immortal symphonies, was deaf. Are you crippled? Alexander Pope was crippled so painfully that he could hardly move, but he became a Goliath of English literature. Are you too young to dream? Linn Yann, a refugee from Southeast Asia who knew no English when she arrived here, became a national spelling bee superstar at the age of 12. Too old? Walter Damrosch wrote and conducted one of his greatest operas when he was 75. Victor Hugo produced his famous *Torquemada* when he was 80. The list goes on and on!

The time to do it is now! Set your booster rocket and push the launching button! With courage and will power, you'll be on your way to your destiny.

Faith and Enthusiasm 29

If you have written down your short- and long-term goals, now it's time to take steps to achieve them. When you work toward your goals, you take one small step at a time, repeating those small steps until you can take bigger steps. It's like going upstairs: you take the first step, the second step, and the third step. You can't go from the first step directly to the third or the fifth step.

These steps can be summed up in the few lines below (reprinted from *The Greatest Salesman in the World,* by Og Mandino. Copyright 1968 by Og Mandino. Used by permission of Frederick Fell Publishers, Inc., Hollywood, Florida.)

I will persist until I succeed.

Henceforth, I will consider each day's effort as but one blow of my blade against a mighty oak. The first blow may cause not a tremor in the wood, nor the second, nor the third. Each blow, of itself, may be trifling, and seem of no consequence. Yet from childish swipes the oak will eventually tumble. So it will be with my efforts of today.

I will be likened to the raindrop which washes away the mountain; the ant who devours a tiger; the star which brightens the earth; the slave who builds a pyramid. I will build my castle one brick at a time for I know that small attempts, repeated, will complete any undertaking.

I will persist until I succeed.

Jump over Hurdles

When you pursue your goals in life, you're like a track-and-field athlete who has to jump over many hurdles. You jump over these hurdles one at a time, not all at once, in a continuing effort. To achieve your goals you must be inspired and enthusiastic.

Jump over Many Hurdles

One example of inspiration is former basketball star "Magic" Johnson whose enthusiasm vibrated among his teammates. He used all his effort, energy, and talent, whether he dribbled the ball, threw a perfect pass to a teammate, or drove toward the basket for a lay-up. He overflowed with enthusiasm; he always smiled, accepted defeats with good humor, and appreciated victories as a team effort. He was a winner!

A man once asked three laborers what they were doing. The first laborer said, "I'm laying a brick." The second laborer gave a similar response. The third laborer said, "I'm building a church!" The third laborer was enthusiastic; he was inspired because he was building a church! And when you're studying, you're not simply reading books and taking notes. You're making your own destiny!

Emulate Vanna White

If you want to be somebody, it's good to have role models. Emulate the movie or TV star (like Vanna White), the painter, the athlete, or the writer you admire. At first copy his or her style of acting, painting, playing, or writing. Later you'll develop a style of your own.

Years ago, a mother took her son to the library to stimulate his interest in baseball. "He would get books about Babe Ruth and Ted Williams," she said "and he would learn through reading. I would read to him first, and then he would read them."

That boy grew up to become the most valuable player in the 1984 World Series, when his team, the Detroit Tigers, clinched the world championship. He was Alan Trammell, the Tigers' shortstop, who also was voted the second most valuable player of the American League in 1987.

Dr. Richard Morales, a psychiatrist and stress-management specialist who practices in Largo, Florida says, "It is necessary to model yourself after others as a more effective way of learning what it is that self-made people do. Find a well-known personality who has done something you admire and read as you can about that person. If there are videotapes of the person, study them so that you can imitate his or her walk and the way he or she talks. Then find out as much as possible about that person's interests."

Smile, Smile, Smile

Build your enthusiasm. Smile and the world smiles with you. Dwell on your past successes, even if they were small, and you'll have more confidence in yourself.

As shown by Asian-Americans who became whiz kids (see their story on pages 237-239), achieving something requires what Thomas Edison called "one percent inspiration and 99 percent perspiration." One percent inspiration is enough. Work hard for your goals, believe that you can achieve them, and you'll succeed.

We are all participants in "races" because we are in competition with other people — whether in class, for jobs, in the workplace, or in business. To beat the competition, you have to catch up with your opponents. Don't stop running. If you look back, someone will pass you.

***Don't Stop Running. If You Look Back,
Someone Will Pass You....***

How can you have faith in yourself or in your goals? Why do you believe you can achieve them?

If you have written down well-planned goals, if you have plans like architects' plans, there's no reason why you can't believe in yourself and in your goals. Besides writing a general statement about what you want to be and when, you must make some affirmations and visualizations.

Emile Coué, a French psychologist, taught his patients to make this affirmation: "Day by day in every way, I am getting better and better!" (His patients did improve!) Tell yourself the same thing. You'll have a good feeling about yourself! You'll feel stronger, more enthusiastic and inspired, and you'll always think positive things.

This kind of self-talk is called *affirmation*. Affirmation is the process by which you talk to yourself, confirming what good things you have done or what good thoughts you have. When these thoughts are repeated again and again, your mind eventually accepts them as true. Then they make you feel good, giving you the enthusiasm and inspiration to push toward your goals.

Seeing Is Believing

The use of affirmations, coupled with visualization, can make your dreams come true. *Visualization* is the process by which you imagine that you are succeeding. If you want to become a scientist, visualize yourself working in a laboratory. See yourself wearing a white coat, looking into the microscope, and trying to figure out what drugs you should discover to fight some kind of disease. See yourself discovering the drug; see yourself being interviewed on television; see yourself on the front page of the newspaper for having discovered an important medicine.

Play and replay these images on the screen of your imagination; feed them to your subconscious mind. If your subconscious mind sees them over and over again, even if they are not yet true, eventually it will believe that they are happening or have happened.

According to psychiatrist Richard Morales, achievers are able to picture themselves where they want to be and experience how it feels to be there. He says, "I call that instant preplay. Transport yourself into a successful experience. See it, hear it, feel it as if it were happening. Then take these fabricated experiences and store them in your memory for reference."

Coming to America

A man named Lyndon Johnson always visualized that he would be in the White House — and he was! When I was little, I always visualized that I would go abroad (maybe to America) — and I did!

Practice affirmations and visualizations every day, especially after you wake up in the morning and before you go to sleep at night. Fill your study room or bedroom with pictures and mottoes such as *If it can be done, I can do it, or Do it now!* In the private offices of many industrial leaders and businessmen are hung such slogans and pictures from great men of the past. F. W. Woolworth, who was called the Napoleon of business, was reported to have a private office that was a replica of Napoleon's study. Leaders like Woolworth did such things to remind themselves that they could suceeed in life just as those great men had succeeded in the past. If you do these things, you'll have constant reminders of your goals and you'll be inspired to act. You won't say "Gimme a Break." You'll make your own breaks! You won't let things happen; you'll make things happen!

30

Persistence and Rewards

Sometime, somewhere, you'll suffer defeats in your endeavors to succeed. At first you may fail in algebra or chemistry, but if you try and try again, you'll make passing grades. You may make even higher grades after you master the formulas, principles, and concepts involved in solving the problems.

Don't let failures deter you; make them your stepping stones to success. Let failures be only *temporary defeats* from which to learn. Don't be afraid to fail, because failures are a test of how tough-minded you are, how much self-discipline you have, and how well you can adjust to any situation. Often, when we admire successful men and women, we see them only when they are already on top; we don't know that they stumbled many times on the way.

Close Your Ears

Close your ears to complainers and persons who often criticize other people. Let the message below be your guide (Reprinted from *The Greatest Salesman in the World,* by Og Mandino. Copyright 1968 by Og Mandino. Used by permission of Frederick Fell Publishers, Inc., Hollywood, Florida):

> I will persist until I succeed.
> I was not delivered unto this world in defeat, nor does failure course in my veins. I am not a sheep waiting to be prodded by my shepherd. I am a lion and I refuse to talk, to walk, to sleep with the sheep. I will hear not those who weep and complain, for their disease is contagious. Let them join the sheep. The slaughterhouse of failure is not my destiny.
> I will persist until I succeed.

Sometimes friends, relatives, and those close to you will judge or criticize you: *Don't do that, you'll only fail! You can't make it as a businessman! You can't make it because no one has ever done it before! If it were a good idea, it would have been done by some-*

body else! Friends and relatives love you, so they don't want you to fail or get hurt, but they don't know that you have your own goals in life and that what you are trying to pursue is attainable. Sometimes, too, some of them are jealous; they don't want you to succeed and leave them behind.

Try again even if you fail! Failure is nothing but a temporary defeat; it is nothing but a chance to learn from your mistakes. Ling Yang, who came here as a refugee and became a high school valedictorian, says, "It is in failure that I learn."

Are you the son or daughter of poor parents who believe that you can't succeed? Years ago one poor boy was too frail to go to school, but his mother taught him to read. He read many books and made a lot of experiments. At first he failed often, but he would not quit. He believed that he could succeed, and he did! This poor boy was James Watt, who invented the steam engine that revolutionized the industrial world. If you believe you can, *you can.*

Thomas Edison suffered thousands of failures while doing his experiments, but he persisted. Every time he failed he discovered one more thing that didn't work. Then all that was left was the only thing that worked. In this way Edison found the path to success and became the world's greatest inventor.

The following verses may sum up one of the laws of success.

You Can

If you think you are beaten, you are,
    If you think you dare not, you don't.
If you like to win, but you think you can't,
    It is almost certain you won't.

If you think you'll lose, you're lost,
    For out in the world we find,
Success begins with a fellow's will—
    It's all in the state of mind.

If you think you are outclassed, you are,
    You've got to think high to rise,
You've got to be sure of yourself before
    You can even win a prize.

Life's battles don't always go
    To the stronger or faster man,
But sooner or later the man who wins
    Is the man WHO THINKS HE CAN!

                                        —Anonymous

Move Forward, Not Backward

If you think you have to make changes in your short- and long-term goals, adjust them to the present situation. As the saying goes, "It's only a fool who doesn't change his mind." Still you must continue to move forward, not backward! Keep your desire ablaze and your faith alive, and always play your "accomplishments" on the screen of your imagination. Then tell yourself, "Go on, go on! You're about to reach your destination!"

Once in a while, when you achieve some large or small success, reward yourself for your accomplishments. If you earned a high grade, dress up, see a movie after class, and have a nice dinner at a good restaurant. Treat yourself well, and you'll feel good about yourself. If you do this every time you succeed, you'll feel successful, as indeed you are!

Seventeen-year-old Meredith Albrecht, a whiz kid who won $7,500 in the 47th Westinghouse Science Search, tells about her family's policy on grades: "Our family works on a grade-reward system, with the pay depending on the level of difficulty and the level of the class. You get $5 for an A in an advanced placement course. If you get a C in a regular course, you have money taken away. Gym grades don't count. None of us ever did well in gym."

So you see, rewards for achievements work!

Life's successes bring small and large rewards. Visualize these rewards; if you have the ambition to be successful in business, imagine the day when you will become rich. If you want to become a good quarterback, see yourself going to the Super Bowl and signing a rich contract, as well as earning millions of dollars from endorsements when you are famous. If you want to become an international pianist, see yourself performing before thousands of people at Carnegie Hall, in Paris, in Vienna, and even in Manila. Climb your ladder to success and find your destiny. Be whatever you want to be!

Climb Your Ladder to Success

Why Asian-Americans Become Whiz Kids **31**

Many Asian-American students, who are children of middle-class people who came to the United States in search of a better life, are doing well in school. For example, they finish far above the average on the math section of the Scholastic Aptitude Test (SAT). In addition, four Asians were among 10 winners of the 47th annual Westinghouse Science Talent Search in 1987. Since 1981, 20 Asian-American students have been among the 70 scholarship winners in this event. Furthermore, a comprehensive study of San Diego-area students showed that the Asian-Americans outscore their peers in high school grade-point averages.

Few TV Hours a Week

Is heredity or hard work the secret of success? The mother of Chetant Nayak, 16, winner of the $20,000 Westinghouse scholarship award, recalls, "When he was young, we let him watch only three or four hours of TV a week, and we chose the programs."

Janet Tseng, a 17-year old from Stuyvesant High School in New York City, won the $15,000 award. Eleven years ago she and her family came to the United States "for better education and opportunities." She says, "My mother really pushed us. She had us do advanced math problems at early ages. Later she showed us newspaper clippings about very intelligent people."

The current population of 5.1 million Asian-Americans represents only 2.1 percent of the total population in the United States. Yet immigrants from the Philippines, China, Korea, Japan, and Vietnam have become the country's most upwardly mobile minority. According to another study, high school students of Asian descent are more likely to go to college — taking more math, science, and foreign language courses — than members of other ethnic groups.

Harold W. Stevenson, a psychology professor at the University of Michigan, states, "It's really unusual for a relatively modest number of people to be so amazingly successful."

Harvard psychology professor Jerome Kagan says, "To put it plainly, they work harder."

Michael Rendor de Guzman, a Filipino-American, has shelves crowded with trophies for citizenship, math, speech, bilingual education, and spelling. He says of his success, "I have this motivation to do really well in class." As a result, he devotes five hours a day to his homework in addition to his other activities.

Because of the success of the Asian-American students, they have been stereotyped as "whiz kids." But some Asian students, particularly refugees from Vietnam, struggle with the new language and often drop out of school.

Hello, America!

Still, there are success stories from Vietnam. When Chau Pham, a refugee from Vietnam who escaped with her mother, brother, aunt, and uncle, arrived in New Orleans in 1980, all she could say in English was "hello." In 1987 Chau, then 17, graduated as valedictorian of Ambramson High School. She had received many scholarships and was a premedical student at Vanderbuilt University when this book was being written. "The worst failure is not trying," she says. "If you try but don't succeed, that's learning."

It seems unfair to compare these Indochinese from Vietnam with children of other Asian parents: Chinese, Filipinos, Japanese, and Koreans. Most of the Vietnamese were not professionals; they came here as refugees, not immigrants, and therefore were not screened. To be accepted as an immigrant one must be a professional: a doctor, an engineer, a nurse, or a member of some other profession (or the husband or wife of a recognized professional). Some Asian immigrants had earned doctorates in their own country. Being professional people, they brought their tradition of self-discipline, patience, determination, and emphasis on education; they are the reason for their children's success .

In a major new coss-cultural study conducted by the University of Michigan's Center for Human Growth and Development, American children were reported to have fallen behind the Taiwanese and Japanese children in reading and mathematics from the day they entered the first grade. The project involved some 1,440 first-

and fifth-graders in three comparable cities, which were judged to represent the mainstream of their cultures: Minneapolis, Taipei (the capital of Taiwan), and Sendai, about 250 miles northeast of Tokyo. The students were given tests in reading, mathematics, and intelligence based on the school curricula in the three countries.

In reading, the Taiwanese were the best in both the first and fifth grades. The Americans had higher vocabulary scores than the Japanese at both levels, and even though the Japanese had higher scores on reading comprehension than Americans in the first grade, they were about equal in the fifth.

In mathematics, the Taiwanese pupils made the highest scores in the first grade and the Japanese in the fifth grade; the Americans placed third at both levels. The Americans accounted for 15 of the 100 top scores and 58 of the bottom 100.

Some Play More, Some Read Less

Among other things, this study showed the following:

- The average school year is shorter in this country — 180 days versus 240 in Japan and Taiwan.

- American students spend less than half as much time as the Chinese and less than two-thirds as much time as the Japanese on academic subjects.

- In class, Americans concentrate less on their work and spend more time talking to each other.

- American students play more, do less homework, and read less after school.

- Japanese and Taiwanese mothers seem to show more interest in academic skills, even with very young children.

As the above examples and studies show, a student's success in school depends on the amount of time he or she spends on studying and homework, the parents' role in academic activities, and the importance that the student attaches to education.

It doesn't matter whether you're a native-born American or an immigrant; what matters is what you do to excel in class or to be an honor student. It's up to you. Learn the effective studying and test-taking techniques and the principles of success in this book, and you'll reach youı destination!

About the Author

How I'm Becoming
What I Want to Be

When I was two years old, my mother died and my father left me in the care of my grandfather and my mother's two sisters so he could marry again. Then one night, he took me in his arms and attempted to carry me out of my grandfather's house, intending not to bring me back again.

My grandfather warned my father, "I would rather see that boy dead than taken out of this house alive!" Of course I lived; I don't know how.

My Early Childhood

I was born on October 31, 1933, in Manila, Philippines, but I grew up in the rural town of General Tinio, Nueva Ecija. At that time, I didn't know or care about my future; I cared only about the present. But before I went to school, I had the time to be alone and to think. My adopted parents were poor farmers, and because of my isolation from society I became a shy boy and a loner. I used to spend the whole day by myself, tending our herds of cattle. I became a cowboy without a horse in the rice fields before and after harvest time.

When I was almost ready to go to school I was taught the English alphabet, because the medium of instruction in school was English, not *Tagalog*, our language. Although I learned first how to speak Tagalog, I learned how to read and write in English before I learned how to read and write in Tagalog. During flag ceremonies before we went to class, we always sang *The Star-Spangled Banner* and *God Bless America*. (At that time we had no national anthem of our own.)

I went through the elementary and intermediate grades without reading a newspaper or encyclopedia, for at that time there were none in my rural hometown. There wasn't a town library, and there wasn't a single radio or TV set, so those inventions didn't distract me from my studies. But without the electric light, another invention that hadn't reached my hometown, I found it hard to study and do my homework; I worked by the flickering light from a crude kerosene-fueled native lamp whose light is like that of a candle. It put me to sleep instead of keeping me awake, whether in the evening or in the middle of the night.

At the age of 18, I went to Manila, the place of my birth, to enter college. From 1951 to 1955 I attended the University of Santo Tomás, where I took a four-year course in journalism. Before I entered the journalism course, however, I spent one year taking pre-medicine because my grandfather wanted me to become a doctor. (Later my grandfather's wish came true, in a way; I married a doctor.)

My dream was to become a writer, to work for a newspaper, and to be an author and publisher someday. But while thousands graduated from journalism programs in Manila, there were only four major national newspapers, three in the English language and one in the national language. Jobs were scarce, so naturally there was too much competition for a newspaper job.

So while still a college student, I figured out that the only chance I had to enter the newspaper world was to take any possible route. I started as a cub reporter, who didn't have a monthly salary but received only a transportation allowance. I asked only for the opportunity to work for the *Bagong Buhay*, a daily newspaper in the national language, and the editor accepted me. Later I was made a member of the editorial staff, as a full-fledged reporter. After four years at the *Bagong Buhay*, I was hired as an English-language newswriter at the radio news station of the Chronicle Broadcasting Network. Then I went to work at the *Manila Chronicle*, a daily English-language newspaper, as a proofreader. Once I was in, I proved myself capable of holding other positions and became a magazine writer, a reporter, and a deskman.

While I was still a reporter, I decided to take a life partner. Thinking that I had found the girl of my dreams, I proposed marriage to Genoveva Abes, a physician, after a one-year engagement. To make this dream a reality, my uncle went to Genoveva's parents to ask for her hand. (My father had died when I was 25 years old.) That's how it's done in the Philippines. My uncle had a problem, however, — not with my would-be mother-in-law, but with my would-be father-in-law. The latter refused my request for Genoveva's hand, saying he could not yet afford to lose one of his children; he had only eleven more.

A cold war began between us but after a year Genoveva's father said "yes." Then we went to the local Catholic church and promised each other never to be separated anymore; we have not forgotten that vow.

During the early years of our marriage I decided to go back to college. With a family to raise and a full-time job as a journalist, I was forced to get some ideas from a book on how to study and learn; I also devised my own system of memorizing and reading. As a result of effective study and test-taking techniques, I made the honor roll in college, for the first time in my life. From then on I exposed my children to books and taught them how to use study techniques in their own schooling. (The results were good; they have excelled in school ever since.)

At age 32 I resigned from my newspaper job to start my own printing business. I wrote to relax and for the love of writing. As a free-lance writer, I was cited as one of the outstanding contributors to the *Philippine Free Press*, an English-language monthly magazine. Expanding my business, I published pupils' and teachers' reference books and teaching aids for the Philippines Department of Education and Culture.

The Discovery of America

On March 13, 1976, my wife and I came, saw, and conquered America. One year later my five children, four boys and one girl, followed us and adopted the mixed culture of the old and the new. Now we are Filipino-Americans.

I've been treated by many doctors in my life, but never by my wife. My first book, *The Book of U.S. Postal Exams*, has been read from cover to cover by thousands of people, but never by my wife. This doesn't mean that we're unhappy with each other, although we are in different fields of endeavor. Like computers, we speak the same language and our software is compatible.

I'm not a neophyte publisher. While I was producing reference books in my native country, I also engaged in the gigantic task of publishing a ten-volume Philippine Encyclopedia. Assembling a

staff of researchers and writers, I successfully crossed geograph-
ical boundaries and convinced well-known anthropologists and
other authorities throughout the world to contribute to the first
volume: *The National Cultural Minorities of the Philippines*, a
book on the history and culture of more than 50 ethnic groups in
the Philippines. I thought that the volume might be a best-seller,
and I invited the country's Secretary of the Department of Education to write the introduction. My editorial staff finished compil-
ing materials and incorporating the works of other authors into a
finished manuscript. Later, however, I realized that I needed millions of pesos to publish an encyclopedia; thus my dream did not
materialize, but I considered it only a temporary defeat. To pursue
our goals in life, my wife and I left the country for the United States
a few years after President Marcos imposed martial law and established his dictatorship.

Although Marcos eventually met his downfall and death, I'm
still alive and kicking. In fact, my hopes are brighter than ever
before.

My wife has been a successful pediatrician, and I think I've
been on the right track to success. I received the national 1990
"Small Press Publisher of the Year Award" from Quality Books
(the largest distributor of nonfiction books to libraries) at the
Publishers Marketing Association reception during the American Booksellers Association convention in Las Vegas. I've also
received six other book awards as an author and a publisher of
nonfiction books, including the book, *The Filipino Americans
(From 1763 to the Present): Their History, Culture, and Tradi-
tions.*

Dreams really come true. So I've not stopped dreaming
dreams. I know that today's accomplishments were yesterday's
dreams, and I believe that I'll fulfill many of my dreams before
The Day After, Que sera, sera, Bahala na! (Whatever will be, will
be!).

Afterword

In this book I've tried to motivate you to have a positive attitude, to set short- and long-term goals, and to ignite the rocket booster for your ambition. I've presented the case histories of average people like myself, who used study and learning skills. Through their courage and commitment they excelled in class and became successful in life.

I didn't have a good educational foundation. I grew up in a rural community in the Philippines at a time when there was no electric light. When I studied at night I used only a crude kerosene-fueled lamp. There was a dearth of books; there were no radio and TV, no motivation, no study skills to learn. Yet in my later life, through goal setting, determination, and the use of study and test-taking techniques, I became a classroom superstar, moved to America, topped the postal exams, and attained my dream of becoming an author. My first work, *The Book of U.S. Postal Exams,* is a silent best-seller and is sold to school and public libraries and through bookstores throughout the United States.

There's nothing you can't do if you want to do it, but you can't do it merely by reading my book. You have to follow the step-by-step instructions; you have to practice every technique I present; you have to motivate yourself, always seeing on the screen of your imagination the person you want to become: a doctor, an engineer, a computer analyst, a writer.

I've given you all the tools for setting and accomplishing goals and for studying and learning. After reading the whole book, go back to every chapter and see that you understand every piece of advice. Let this book be your guide in every way, every day, as you travel the route to your destiny! Let the story of every boy or girl, man or woman, in this book be your inspiration, wherever you go and whatever you do. I know you can do it, because it has been done! It's up to you. Should you improve your grades or become an honor student, please let us know. You may be qualified for an achievement award that we give to students of all ages who have become super achievers with the help of this book. Write to **Bookhaus Publishers,** P.O. Box 1758, Warren, MI 48090-1758.

Veltisezar B. Bautista
Author

Bibliography and Recommended Reading

Armstrong, William H. and Willard Lampe II. *Study Tips: How to Study Effectively and Get Better Grades.* Barron's Educational Series, Woodbury, NY.

Beck, Joan. "Can't America Build Better Brains?" *Detroit Free Press,* June 27, 1986.

Bliss, Edwin C. *Doing It Now.* Charles Scribner's Sons, New York, NY.

Bristol, Claude M. *The Magic of Believing.* Pocket Books/Simon and Schuster, New York.

Buzan, Tony. *Make the Most of Your Mind.* Linden Press/Simon and Schuster, New York.

The Diagram Group. *The Brain: A User's Manual.* Perigee Books/ G.P. Putnam's Sons, New York.

Engleman, Siegfried and Therese. *Give Your Child a Superior Mind.* Cornerstone Library/Simon and Schuster, New York.

Green, Gordon W. *Getting Straight A's.* Lyle Stuart, Inc., Secaucus, NJ.

Hammer, Signe, "The Brain is Nearly a Chemical Soup." *Science Digest,* October 1985.

Healy, Jane M. "Brain Power." *Parents Magazine,* December 1986.

Herold, Mort. *Memorizing Made Easy.* Contemporary Books, Chicago.

Hill, Napoleon. *Think and Grow Rich.* Ballantine Books/Random House, New York.

Huffhines, Kath. "Hispanic Films Bank Insight with Profits." *Detroit Free Press,* April 17, 1988.

Kunerth, Jeff. "Americans Think Highly of IQ Tests," *Detroit Free Press,* October 29, 1985.

Lapointe, Joe. "MVP in 1984?" *Detroit Free Press,* May 20, 1984.

Loray, Harry and Jerry Lucas. *The Memory Book.* Ballantine Books/Random House, New York.

Lord, Lew and Nancy Limon, "What Puts the Whiz in Whiz Kids." *U.S. News & World Report,* March 14, 1988.

Maddox, Harry. *How to Study.* Fawcett Premier Books/CBS, New York.

Mandino, Og. *The Greatest Salesman in the World.* Bantam Books, New York.

Maranto, Gina. "The Mind within the Brain," *Discover,* May 1984.

Martindale, M.L. "To Get Rich, Think as the Rich Do." *Detroit Free Press,* May 1, 1988.

Milan, Jason and Walter Pauk. *How to Take Tests,* McGraw-Hill, New York.

Minninger, Joan. *Total Recall.* Rodale Press, Emmaus, PA.

Reagan, Ron. "To Know a Genius." *Parade Magazine,* October 2, 1983.

Schwartzberg, Neala. "Bright, Average, or Slow?" *Parents Magazine,* May 1987.

Stone, W. Clement. *The Success System That Never Fails.* Pocket Books/Simon and Schuster, New York.

"Those Asian-American Whiz Kids." *Time,* August 31, 1987.

Trimer, Margaret. "Moua Yang," *Detroit Free Press,* June 7, 1987.

Wit, Daniel and P. Allan Dionisopoulos. *American Government and Political System.* Glencoe/McGraw-Hill, Mission Hills, CA.

Yepson, Roger B. Jr. *How to Boost Your Brain Power.* Rodale Press, Emmaus, PA.